THE STOCK MARKET
CRASH OF 1929

THE
STOCK MARKET
CRASH OF 1929

by
GORDON V. AXON

 Mason & Lipscomb PUBLISHERS   NEW YORK

Copyright © Mason & Lipscomb Publishers, Inc. 1974

Published simultaneously in the United Kingdom by Mason & Lipscomb,
London, England.

Library of Congress Catalog Card Number: 74-3409

International Standard Book Number: 0-88405-074-2

First Printing

Printed in the United States of America

Library of Congress Cataloging in Publication Data

Axon, Gordon V
    The stock market crash of 1929.

    Bibliography: p.
    1. Depressions--1929--United States. 2. Stock-
exchange. 3. United States--Economic conditions--1918-
1945. I. Title.
HB3717 1929.A96   330.9'73'091   74-3409
ISBN 0-88405-074-2

For Nell, Margaret, Jackie, and Jill

Contents

PART II: FOR DISCUSSION

List of Illustrations

PART 1

THE STOCK MARKET CRASH OF 1929

1. United States: Financial Center of the World

TODAY, WHEN WE THINK of 1929, the subject that comes most readily to mind is the stock market crash. Just as 1941 is remembered for the day of infamy at Pearl Harbor, so 1929 has etched itself into the American memory as the beginning of unparalleled financial disaster in Wall Street.

The Stock Market Crash of 1929 ranks as the most shocking financial event in the history of the United States. Although booms and collapses had been known before in Wall Street, and have been seen since, the events of 1929 are unique. Stock prices were so high and conditions were such in that year that when prices of securities began to tumble they brought down with them the whole business structure. This collapse helped bring on the Great Depression, and it ushered in a new era of government regulation of stock exchanges that was to provide much greater protection for investors.

The story, of course, does not begin in 1929. Rather it starts in 1776, when the American colonies broke away from the mother country and became independent. At that time the fledgling republic had only a few million inhabitants. Even by 1860 the United States was not important as a source of loan capital in the world's financial markets; she had to borrow money abroad for her own industrial development. This money came mainly from London, which was the financial capital of the world throughout the 19th century.

London ruled the world's financial roost. From London flowed the capital to finance construction of railroads, factories, ports, and all kinds of business and commercial activities in the British Empire and other parts of the world.

How did Britain obtain so much capital? It came from the savings of the British people and from foreign investments that had proved successful. Over several generations, a huge pool of capital had been formed from which economic activity in Britain and abroad could be financed.

By the second half of the 19th century, however, Britain's domination of the world financial scene was being challenged. Other nations were growing both industrially and financially. And of these, no country had more potential than the United States. Even in 1860, she was destined to become the world's most important business and financial power.

Achieving that power took time. The Civil War, or the War between the States, gave industry an enormous boost. In succeeding decades the country was opened up by the construction of thousands of miles of railroads. The population grew enormously, largely as a result of vast immigration, mainly from Europe. Farms and factories turned out an increasing variety of goods. By the beginning of the 20th century, the United States had become a world industrial power.

This meant prosperity for the American people. It meant savings. Not that each family could save up much, but financial and industrial institutions saved up as well. In short, the United States was following in the footsteps of Britain, a nation already highly developed industrially.

There was one major difference, though, stemming from the two countries' great difference in size. Britain could afford to export her capital to other lands in the form of investments, since she did not need to keep all her savings at home for economic development. The United States, on the other hand, was busily developing her own vast territory. She needed money for many things, including plantations, farms, factories, houses, railroads, water supply facilities, and industrial equipment. Little capital could be spared for investment abroad since there were so many good opportunities available in the United States.

But this too was gradually changing, as more and more of the financial houses in Wall Street turned to Europe. In addition to investing in American industry and agriculture, the Wall Street financiers became increasingly interested in foreign investments as capital became more abundant at home. New York, in short, was gradually becoming the financial capital of the world, supplanting London.

The actual switch from London to New York came about in 1914 when Europe was suddenly plunged into conflict by the outbreak of World War I. Until that time, Britain and other major nations were on the gold standard. Gold actually circulated as currency, but when war broke out in 1914, Britain could no longer afford the luxury of being on the gold standard. The gold was required to finance Britain's war effort and to pay for imports of foods and military equipment. So Britain, in effect, went off the

London *Times* for August 5, 1914. When Britain declared war on Germany in 1914, she in effect went off the gold standard, and the status of world financial leader passed to Wall Street. *Courtesy London Times.*

gold standard. Also, for war reasons, Britain had to temporarily restrict her foreign investment to the British Empire. Wall Street became the financial center of the world.

By 1918, when peace returned to Europe, no other nation could compete with the United States for the position of world's financial leader.

Britain clearly remained second to the United States—even when, for a few postwar years, Britain and other nations went back on the gold standard (actually it was the gold exchange standard, since gold coins did not circulate but gold was used to settle international debts).

The war resulted in much more than a shift in financial power. It ravaged or weakened all of the major countries of Europe. Britain, France, Germany, Russia, Austria-Hungary, Italy—all of them suffered greatly in terms of casualties, economic losses and the great expense of waging war for four years. The United States, which entered the war in 1917, was luckier. Her land had not been occupied or made into a battlefield, she had not suffered the loss of millions of her fighting men, her factories and cities and farms had not been destroyed, her overseas investments had not been sold to pay for military equipment. By 1918 America's allies owed her billions of dollars for having financed much of the war effort. Both at home and abroad, the country had been successful. So it was that the United States emerged from World War I with much of the world's gold and as the acknowledged leader of the Western world.

Small wonder that a sense of national optimism prevailed among Americans in the postwar years. This spirit of confidence and hope, and a real pride in being American, quickly reflected themselves in a booming economy based on widespread industrial and agricultural development. But vast changes in social and political thinking also were occurring in America. Some of these came from across the Atlantic and as a result of the war. One of the most important stemmed from the wartime collapse of Russia and the subsequent takeover by the communists. The Soviet Union was immediately regarded in the Western world as a threat to capitalism.

The very presence of a huge communist power was enough to frighten many westerners. Before long, a state of near hysteria prevailed in the United States, especially when socialism and radicalism were seen to be taking root. Communists and radicals were viewed with horror. They were the ones most frequently blamed for unexplained crimes and acts of violence. So when a huge explosion echoed through Wall Street on Thursday, September 16, 1920, it was viewed by many people as a communist attack on the very citadel of American finance and the world capitalist system. The explosion occurred just outside the United States Assay Office and near the building occupied by one of the country's most prominent financial houses, the J. P. Morgan & Company. About forty people were killed immediately or died later, and some three hundred were injured.

Who caused the lethal blast? It could have been the work of communist plotters or some lunatic. It could even have been an accident, in that many buildings in the area were then being demolished to make way for skyscrapers. Despite extensive investigations, however, the reasons for the explosion have remained a mystery for more than fifty years. And the pockmarks in the walls of the Morgan building are there to this day.

Scene in Wall Street on September 16, 1920, just after the explosion near offices of J. P. Morgan & Company. *Courtesy Morgan Guaranty Trust Company*.

Wall Street was shaken by the disaster but recovered quickly. It was already on the long road of success and heady prosperity that brought about growing speculation in securities and finally the stock market boom that collapsed so ignominiously in a shambles in 1929.

The stock market, of course, is the center for the buying and selling of securities. Many varieties of securities exist, the two main types being bonds and stocks (a bond represents a loan by an investor to a company; a stock represents the investor's part-ownership in a company). Most investors prefer stocks to bonds, since stocks, as a group, provide a way of participating in business growth. In addition, stocks often bring rising dividend income and capital gains, and they are often a hedge against the type of inflation that completely destroys such investments as bank deposits and bonds.

The stock market itself has several parts since securities are traded in many places. Transactions do not have to go through an organized stock exchange. In the popular mind, though, the stock market is Wall Street, and Wall Street is the New York Stock Exchange.

Certainly that was the case just after World War I. The nation was beginning to develop such a head of speculative steam that, when the financial explosion came in 1929, Wall Street was far more shattered than it was by the bomb blast in 1920.

In the postwar period, the New York Stock Exchange was very much a private club, often with more consideration for its members than for the investing public. Not that the public could not make sound investments and obtain a good return on its money, but the cards were stacked against it. Too many insiders, speculators who had secret or inside information about companies, operated very actively in the stock market. Prices were forced up and forced down ruthlessly. It was important in those days to know who was rigging what stock. Many small investors would hang around brokerage offices and listen for hot tips, many of which were being spread by the big operators who bought and sold respectably through members of the New York Stock Exchange. In this procedure, known as rigging, the big boys of Wall Street told the small boys to buy when the big boys wished to get rid of the very securities they had earlier bought from other small investors. Consequently, small operators often lost every penny. Nevertheless, a small investor lucky enough to pick the right stock at the right time could make a fortune on very little capital.

Today, as we look back at what then happened in the period after World War I, we tend only to see inside operators rigging the market and small investors being taken for a ride. We see the shocking use of the stock market machinery to cheat the public. We see the members of the stock exchange using their power to wipe out small fry. We see the aristocracy of finance gaining vast wealth at the expense of the working man.

This view, though, is accurate for only part of the time and in the case of only some securities. It is not the whole story by any means. Probably the vast bulk of all transactions in the decade before the crash in 1929 occurred at prices considered reasonably fair by both buyer and seller. It was a free market, often an exciting market, but one in which the insider and the member of the stock exchange had considerable advantage over the ordinary investor.

The market moved up and down day after day, month after month, and year after year—just as it does now. But few investors in the years before 1929 ever thought that Wall Street would collapse as it did, or that the economy would and stagnate as it did, during the Great Depression, with millions of people out of work.

The early 1920s were a time of booming industry, of soaring hope and confidence. The ups and downs of the stock market were hardly noticed by the average busy American, since he simply was not interested in stocks at that time. It was largely a professional market in that most of the transactions in Wall Street were for big investors who knew the ropes and usually were well financed.

Only later in the decade, when the stock market was

really roaring, did small investors, as a group, take an active role—a role that grew enormously by 1929. Many such investors were simply gambling, putting down a hundred dollars or so and often being wiped out the same day or within a day or two. A few, of course, rode a rising market and managed to keep much of what they made until the 1929 crash wiped them out too.

The speculative tempo gradually increased. A crash such as that in 1929 could not have occurred without a huge build-up in public interest over many years. A vast speculative position was slowly accumulated as more and more investors saw the stock market as a place in which to get rich quickly.

By 1929, a speculative mood was rampant among Americans. The stock market was a main topic of discussion all over the United States. Many people had come to believe that prosperity would last forever and that stock prices would never seriously decline. Almost no one expected a major collapse in the stock market that would later be accompanied by an industrial depression and by a breakdown of the banking system. Even now, 1929 and succeeding years seem almost a nightmare. Stock prices had risen so high that, when the tide turned, nothing could stop the deluge of selling as small investors by the thousands were sold out by their brokers who themselves often did not know the prices at which stocks were being traded. But the brokers did know that their customers had long since lost their margin (the deposit they had paid to buy securities). The customers had been cleaned out. Their securities had to be sold for whatever they would bring.

So many transactions took place in days of hectic selling that the tape machine recording the transactions often ran hours late. Brokers were selling stocks without even knowing what price the stocks were likely to bring.

It was not only that investors lost their deposits; often they ended up owing money—far more money, in fact, than they had originally placed on deposit. Even the big operators in Wall Street, and the big bankers and brokerage houses, were deeply wounded financially. Many were forced into bankruptcy—and thereby out of business.

The abrupt end to the era of confidence shook Wall Street and the nation for years. Decades passed before many stocks again reached their high price of 1929. Some never did, since the companies went out of business or were taken over by more successful firms.

Without doubt, the stock market crash of 1929 ranks as one of the great events in world history because by 1929 the United States was the acknowledged leader of world trade, business, and finance.

2. The Stock Market in an Expanding Economy

THE STOCK MARKET does not exist in a vacuum. It is part and parcel of society. Those that invest in securities are simply citizens going about their business in the usual way. They may be financiers in Wall Street, importers and exporters, professional men and women, farmers, or industrial workers. In short, what goes on in Wall Street reflects the hopes and fears of the country as a whole.

An investor who is fully employed is far more likely to be optimistic than one who is out of work. A businessman who is making profits will feel far more hopeful about the economy and the stock market than one who is losing money because of poor trade. Stock prices, then, are determined by the spirit of the people that buy and sell securities.

To understand how stock prices rose to such heights by 1929, we must turn back to the years immediately after World War I. Nothing as momentous as the crash of 1929 could possibly have developed in a short time. A full decade

Four Generations of Tickers. The model at top, right, was in use in 1929. The first stock market ticker (top, left) was invented in 1867 by E. A. Calahan and remained in use until 1883, when it was replaced by the one at top, right, which was developed by Thomas A. Edison. Its glass dome became a symbol of the Exchange and Wall Street. With modifications, the Edison ticker attained a speed of 285 characters a minute. In 1930 it was succeeded by the ticker shown at lower left, which has a speed of 500 characters a minute. Another version of the ticker (at lower right) came out in 1964 and operates at speeds up to 900 characters a minute. *Courtesy New York Stock Exchange.*

passed after the war before the speculative mania reached its climax.

During this postwar period, the economy and the stock market suffered ups and downs. No steady gradual movement upward occurred. Indeed, there was a severe economic depression immediately after the war, but this did not last long. Seen in retrospect, it does not look too important when compared with that of the 1930s.

By the fall of 1921, a boom had begun to replace the sharp economic setback of the previous 12 months. Interest rates began to fall, and business felt encouraged to expand (since the cost of borrowing capital is one of the major costs of being in business). Corporations were further encouraged by cuts in taxes, since this means that more of the earnings can be ploughed back into the business or paid out as dividends to investors. The automobile industry, able to sell all the cars it could produce, was but one of many industries that greatly expanded production.

The shipyards also were prospering, as they had during the war when so many ships, freighters and warships, were needed for many things, including selling goods abroad, shipping arms and men to the war fronts, and protecting the sea lanes. For years after World War I, American shipyards were kept busy, since so many vessels were needed to transport the goods bought heavily by nations that needed to replenish their stocks of food, industrial raw materials, and machinery. Many of these goods were transported in foreign bottoms, as ships are sometimes referred to, but so many ships had been sunk during the war that many nations were only too willing to pay for the use of American ships, even though freight charges are usually much higher in American than in foreign bottoms. In turn, American shipyards were kept busy building freighters.

So many parts of American industry were booming in those early postwar years that boom is an accurate description of the economy. The stock market, of course, usually anticipates or moves ahead of business conditions. The stock market was rising in 1919—well ahead of the postwar industrial boom. Brokers were kept busy running around trying to fill all their orders to buy stocks. But most Americans simply were not interested in speculation then. Quite often, the volume of business on the New York Stock Exchange was less than one million shares daily, only a fraction of what it is today or was in 1929. The public did not care. Investing in stocks was mainly the preoccupation of wealthy and professional people.

The financial columns of newspapers that are so comprehensive today did not exist then. A column or two was enough for all stock prices, while the specialized financial and business news was hardly given a thought by the average American. The fantastic speculation of the late 1920s was still far away. The stock market was very definitely used mainly by the well-to-do and not by the general public.

Heavy buying of popular stocks gave them quite a boom in the spring of 1919. General Motors shares, for instance, rose by 50 percent. Shipping shares were even more popular in Wall Street; some shipping stocks doubled in price in a few months.

The booming market anticipated the business advance of 1920. But the economy soon turned down and dropped very sharply indeed in late 1920 and 1921. The upward turn came, as it always does, but in 1922 and 1923 the advance was unsteady. The economy fell off again in 1924 and 1927, but these declines were nothing much and were shrugged off both by business and the general public.

By 1928, the hesitations of the early postwar years were obviously over. The country was gaining in confidence and economic strength. Wall Street had become accustomed to its new title of world financial leader, which it had gained unexpectedly in 1914 when Britain both forsook the gold standard and stringently limited the investment of funds overseas.

In the late 1920s, the business of America was truly business. Wall Street and Main Street participated. Some sectors of the economy were being hurt by various factors. Cheap imports, for instance, restricted shoe and textile manufacturing. Business in general, however, was profitable and expanding. A major factor in this economic advance was the rapid growth of two new industries which created thousands of jobs. The automobile was an almost instant favorite with Americans. Between 1919 and 1929, for instance, the number of cars on the road rose by over 200 percent. Millions of people saved up almost desperately for their first car. Many families preferred a car to a good home, probably because of the lower cost involved but also because ownership of a car created mobility, a sense of power, and a feeling of equality and pride.

The other new industry was radio production. This industry was newer than the automobile industry, and, radio prices being lower than those for cars, the demand for radios was even greater. Radio broadcasting was unknown in 1919, but began in 1920 and had generated enormous public enthusiasm by 1922. Between 1922 and 1929, the dollar value of radio sales rose every year except 1927, when the economy declined. The biggest boom in radio sales occurred in the first few years, when few families had radios. Sales in 1923, for instance, were more than double those for 1922, and sales in 1924 were well over double those in 1923. In fact, sales in 1924 were about six times greater than those in 1922. Although annual sales increases

The radios of 1928 reflected the opulence of the age. Here is a Radiola 60. *Courtesy RCA.*

after that were not as large, radio sales in 1929 represented an overall increase of 1300 percent since 1922 and were approaching the $1-billion figure. Small wonder that the common stock of the Radio Corporation of America (commonly called Radio by investors) became a favorite in Wall Street.

The U.S. economy, of course, depended on much more

than one or two products during the 1920s. Nevertheless, it was these two booming industries—automobile and radio manufacture—that played a major role in stimulating a steady and general business advance. They directly provided jobs for thousands, and indirectly for many more since the prosperity of any industry spills over as workers spend their wages and the industry itself buys plant and equipment. The automobile, for instance, needs gasoline and oil. Motorists require filling stations and restaurants.

Most industries shared in the business expansion. The growing prosperity brought rising demand for electrical devices, such as telephones and refrigerators. People had money for the movies. The wide variety of goods sold in chain stores gave that business a boom. Retail trade in general expanded greatly; for example, while women bought cosmetics and rayon stockings and underwear, men (and later many women) purchased cigarettes and cars.

Thus, with few exceptions, American industry grew mightily during the 1920s. The setback in 1924, and that in 1927, caused trouble for some firms and individuals, but the general economic trend was upward. As the economy roared along, so stock prices advanced and public interest in the stock market grew. Companies made large profits, and the dividends they paid their stockholders increased.

Even better times were anticipated. The stock market gradually but surely became the focal point of interest for millions of Americans who had grown accustomed to prosperity and expected it to continue forever.

The idea of unlimited and undiminished prosperity seems rather ridiculous now, but that is hindsight. At the time, many reasons were given for everlasting business growth. The United States, for instance, clearly had the world's greatest economy. Better than any other nation, she had developed machines for the mass production of a great variety of goods. People felt confident about the future and no longer always bought goods for cash; instead, they often paid for their purchases on the installment system. Thus many less-than-affluent families could afford items worth a good share of a year's income, or even more.

The rising stock market also helped generate a feeling of acquired wealth among investors. In the early years of the boom, few Americans had an investment in Wall Street, but the number of investors rose as stock prices advanced. Such holders of securities naturally felt better off when their investments soared in price. Their capital had increased and no doubt they used some of the stock market profits to buy automobiles, possibly new homes.

The general prosperity also gave great impetus to the importance of two activities that had not attracted much attention before. For instance, the advertising of goods, especially on radio, created a huge demand for certain products almost overnight. Salesmen, on radio and elsewhere, often became the key to business success, while advertising itself quickly acquired the status almost of a new industry.

The decade of the 1920s was one of hope, not of fear. It started off with doubt and hesitation, but quickly became an era of staggering success as prosperity extended to millions of American families the privileges previously reserved for the rich.

Social barriers fell as, compared with the rest of the world, the United States became a middle-class country. Poverty existed then and still does, but more and more

Automobile demand gave impetus to economic boom in the 1920s. A 1920 Ford Model T Roadster is seen here along with a car that got stuck in the mud. *Courtesy Educational Affairs Department, Ford Motor Company.*

Americans were able to obtain a good education and a fine start to life. They felt freer than any other people in history, partly because the automobile made them physically mobile and partly because class distinctions declined as affluence spread.

Americans no longer were hemmed in physically, socially, mentally, or even morally. This, of course, is an exaggeration if taken at face value, but the difference, in feeling and attitudes, between the decade before World War I and that after it is surely one of the most marked in U.S. history. The decade leading up to 1929 was an era of revolution in ideas, beliefs, inventions, and ways of living. It included the noble experiment of Prohibition, jazz, the vote for women, the trial of Sacco and Vanzetti, scandals in government, the flapper age, the boom in crossword puzzles, and the achievements of Charles A. Lindbergh.

Much, of course, has occurred since. Today, the pace of accelerating change is bewildering to many, but the sobering events of the stock market crash and Depression, followed as they were by World War II and the long postwar boom, put the events of the 1920s in perspective. We see now how the success of the United States in World War I, coupled with the prostration of much of Europe, created the conditions for business boom, general prosperity, and stock market speculation and collapse. We also see now how high unemployment and low wages brought despair in Europe and the rise of dictators such as Hitler and Mussolini. In turn, World War II became inevitable as each country looked after its own interests and refused joint efforts against aggression.

The story of social change in that decade is fantastic

enough, as is that of the business developments and inventions that now are taken for granted. But the most unbelievable of all is what went on in Wall Street—how the stock market operated, and how a stock market crash became possible, indeed inevitable, once the boom had passed the point of no return in the final fling of 1928 and 1929.

3. Rigging the Market

TODAY, MUCH OF THE TRADING in stocks and bonds is done by the big financial institutions, such as mutual funds, insurance companies, pension funds, and banks that look after the investments of their customers. In the 1920s, though, most of the buying and selling of stocks was done by private investors, often wealthy people. Quite frequently, pools (of money) were organized so that particular stocks could be forced up or down in price.

It is still possible today to buy or sell heavily in order to force prices in one direction or another. Usually, however, price moves are the result of normal buying and selling. A stock may become attractive for many reasons. Investors hear the news and buy. Others read the newspapers and wonder why the stock is going up—so they too rush in and buy. Likewise, stocks may drop on bad news. By and large, and with very few exceptions, the price movements seen in the stock market today result generally from buying and selling on the part of investors.

In the 1920s, this was not always the case. Life was much freer then for speculators who wished to rig the market.

25

Indeed, Wall Street regarded it as none of government's business to step in and control speculation.

Nor could the government have done much even had it so desired. The government at the federal level was then limited in its ability to control the stock market. It possessed very few powers to intervene in the financial markets. In fact, strange though it may seem today, the federal government itself often borrowed through private bankers.

In a financial crisis, such as a loss in the nation's gold reserves or in a bank panic, the government often turned to private bankers for advice and possibly financial assistance. The basic reason for this, of course, was the then much greater importance of Wall Street as a financial center, in relation to the financial needs of the federal government. Today, the federal government's need for money is so great that Wall Street is much less important a factor in supplying it than it was early in the century and even after World War I.

There was little government supervision over the securities business during the 1920s. Manipulation of prices by unscrupulous speculators was commonplace. They often would band together and work in unison to force up or down the prices of particular stocks.

Speculators also could operate by themselves. For a small down payment, a speculator could buy one hundred shares. He might put down $100 or $200 as a deposit on a transaction involving several times as much. This was legal but risky to the speculator, since the broker through which he bought took good care to protect his own interests.

Naturally enough, a decline in the price of the stock often wiped out speculators who had put down only a small deposit. That was because the broker watched stock prices carefully. He kept a note of which investors had bought which stocks and at what price, and, if a stock dropped below a certain level, the broker would sell the stock, creating a loss for the speculator. In some cases, the speculator lost all his deposit and even might owe the broker a balance. In other cases, his deposit was substantially reduced by the loss on the transaction.

One shady method used by some speculators in the 1920s was the so-called wash sale. A wash sale is bogus. Even though wash sales were illegal, they occurred all the same. Such bogus sales were used to create the illusion of public interest in a stock. This would often generate more buying, which in turn would drive up the price of the stock.

How does a wash sale work?

Let us say that a stock is selling for around $15, and that there is little public enthusiasm for it, but that four speculators—A, B, C, D—feel that it has something to offer. It is just a matter of getting the price moving up, of spreading rumors, and of then unloading the stock onto an unsuspecting public at a profit.

So the speculators form a pool, which starts buying at $15 a share and manages to push the price up to $20 and then to $25. The pool buys 100,000 shares, paying an average price of $20 per share. That is $2 million in capital, much of it no doubt borrowed. This kind of thing happened all the time in the 1920s. But since many pools were operating in the stock market at the same time, much effort was often needed to get the public interested in a particular stock. Furthermore, the price would have to be forced much higher than $25 for the pool to make a profit, the reason being that a pool that is unloading on the market forces the price down as it sells, just as it forced the price up when it bought. So the market price must be much more than $25 when the pool's selling begins.

So the four speculators then make wash sales. Rather than selling their stock on the open market, they simply pass their shares of stock among themselves at prearranged rising prices. Such a pool could operate on much less capital than if genuine buying and selling took place.

So speculator A sells 1,000 shares to B at $26 a share. Actually, no genuine transaction takes place—B does not have to pay A. Then B sells the shares to C at $27. In turn, C sells them to D at $28, and D sells them back to A at $29. This can go on indefinitely.

The public does not know what is going on and simply concludes that someone in the know is buying heavily. So it rushes in and buys, which helps force the price higher and higher. Other investors see what is happening and they too wish to get in on a good thing. Rumors are spread by the pool; for example, that the dividend paid on the stock will be increased. So more buyers rush in.

Finally, the pool is ready to sell on the market. By that time, the public is buying without thinking. The pool unloads gently at first, since many investors hope to buy on a setback in the price. The price drops, and, sure enough, more investors give orders to buy.

The pool then gets rid of most of its holdings, simply throwing them onto the market and finally winding up with a handsome profit.

This sort of thing—a wash sale—happened all the time in the years leading up to the Wall Street crash of 1929.

Sometimes, of course, the stock market was falling. This condition encouraged what were known as short selling, short sales, and bear raids. These were attempts by sellers to force the price down and to terrify the public into selling. The bears would then buy back the shares they had earlier borrowed and sold at higher prices.

Say that a pool operating a bear raid has borrowed, for a fee, 100,000 shares. The pool begins to sell and the price drops. The public panics, and the price falls from, say, $20 to $10 a share. The pool then buys back.

Quite often, pools would churn the market, quite apart from carrying out bear raids. They would buy, for instance, hoping to sell at a profit. Or they would sell heavily, then buy heavily if they felt confident of making a net profit on their total transactions. The actions of the pools depended to a large extent on how the public and other speculators responded to the movements in the market prices of securities.

Naturally enough, many speculators tried to protect themselves against losing too much money. They did this by setting stop orders, sometimes known as stop-loss orders, that helped limit their losses.

A speculator, for instance, might buy 1,000 shares at $20 a share and put in a stop order to sell at $15. This means that his stockbroker would sell if, but only if, the price fell and hit $15. If the price continued to rise, all would be well; eventually, the speculator would sell his stock and take a profit. But if the price started falling, his broker would sell the shares as soon as the price of that stock appeared on the ticker tape at $15.

In this way, one sale would trigger another sale. One speculator may have bought at $21 and put a stop order to sell at $17. Another speculator may have bought at $22 and, being cautious, put a stop order to sell at $19. So a small decline in price could easily trigger a wave of selling as one stop order after another was touched off as the price fell.

This process was known to pool operators as triggering the stops. In fact, it still happens today.

This, then, was the way some people speculated in stocks during the 1920s—and even long before World War I. Wash sales, bear raids, frenzied buying and selling—it all seems chaotic, and it was. Day after day, week after week, month after month, and year after year, this sort of

The floor of the now American Stock Exchange when the former street market, known as the Curb, built its own exchange in 1921. *Courtesy American Stock Exchange.*

speculation occurred on the New York Stock Exchange as the early years following World War I rolled on into the mid-1920s and beyond.

The buying and selling of stocks took place, of course, in the usual way in the offices of stockbrokers. Many speculators and even some investors put down only a small fraction of the total cost and hoped that stocks would move quickly in the right direction. Other buyers would purchase stocks as an investment, simply buying them and locking them up in their safes. On balance, these investors fared very well up to 1929, since the stock market saw generally rising prices.

Periodically, though, the stock market would fall heavily, wiping out many speculators. Some of them would come back in the next boom, however, and the process would repeat itself. Some of the more successful speculators would pyramid their winnings, building an upside-down financial pyramid on a very small capital base. A market setback could wipe out the entire structure, since the financial foundations were built on making small deposits for large amounts of stock.

As the years passed, the speculation became more frantic as the public joined in the fun. By the mid-1920s, the fever of stock market gambling was beginning to affect, even infect, millions of Americans who wished to dabble in the market, hoping to make at least a modest profit.

These were the days when watching the ticker tape giving details of stock market transactions gradually grew into a public mania. People learned how to read the tape, or so they said. The ticker machine printing out the tape became an obsession throughout the land. Stocks were bought on small margins and large hopes.

No doubt all this had some impact on the economy and on the financial structure of the country. The economy rose and fell, and so did the stock market. Businesses sometimes prospered, then had difficult times. Banks would experience panics, and some would go bankrupt, causing heavy personal losses among their depositors. Some investors made fortunes, others lost them. It was all taken in stride by the American public.

The possibility of a stock market crash was not taken too seriously. After all, there had been crashes every now and again for generations in one country or another. And although the U.S. crashes had been followed by, or even caused by, business failures or banking panics, the economy had always got up again, so to speak, and moved ahead to bigger things as the population grew and the nation developed economically.

So it was that most Americans in the 1920s looked upon prosperity as something stretching endlessly into the future. The public was buying. The insiders were operating. The last surge of the great bull market of the 1920s had begun. Few people realized that the stage had been set for the greatest market crash of all.

4. The Economic Boom of the 1920s

A QUICK BUT THOROUGH LOOK at the economic progress of the United States after World War I provides a clear understanding of how the concept of perpetual business prosperity, which helped generate the stock market boom in the late 1920s, developed after 1924.

In 1914, Europe was plunged into war. The United States was intent on keeping out, and President Woodrow Wilson asserted that the war would not affect the American people. Nevertheless, the United States was bound by many ties to the Old World, especially since she was the most important of the neutral nations.

The first shock of war did little to help the United States, but the nation soon realized that American industry would benefit. Confidence quickly returned as the Allies in Europe bought the vast variety of U.S. goods they needed to fight the war and feed their people.

American exports to Europe nearly doubled between 1914 and 1915, and rose 50 percent more in 1916. By

1917, the United States also was at war. It was a struggle financed by highly inflationary means, and, even though the war did not last long in terms of direct U.S. involvement, America's postwar economy had to adjust to the absence of heavy military outlays.

Nearly all the armed forces were demobilized within a year of the Armistice of November 11, 1918, and, in the early part of 1919, business activity turned sharply downward. Nevertheless, it quickly rose again in a postwar boom that lasted nearly a year.

In the second half of 1920, postwar inflation gave way to a recession and business was bad. In the next twelve months, wholesale prices fell by one third, unemployment rose to nearly five million, industrial output dropped by a quarter, businesses were plunged into bankruptcy by the tens of thousands, and, within a few years, hundreds of thousands of farmers had been forced off the land by falling farm prices.

Deflation had replaced inflation. Industry suffered. Commodities such as wheat and wool fell in price by more than half.

Action was taken to reverse the business trend. The so-called farm bloc in Congress passed the Emergency Tariff Act of 1921 under which the import duties on corn, wheat, meat, wool, and sugar were raised. In 1922, the Congress passed a law giving the United States its highest import duties in peacetime; commodities and manufactured goods were included.

These moves, designed to help American farmers and industry, did not achieve all their goals. The farmers, for instance, were no better off, in that food surpluses kept prices down. Also, the higher import duties, which raised the prices of foreign food, brought no relief to American farmers since foreign food already cost more than that produced at home.

Industry recovered, however, and, except for farmers, prosperity gradually became general. In the deflationary period, businesses had in stock a large amount of goods paid for at much higher prices. It took time to get rid of these inventories, and losses were often taken on the sales. Pig iron production, for instance, fell by over 70 percent between August 1920 and July 1921. Exports declined by nearly one half in the same period. Retail food prices fell by nearly one third, and farm crop prices dropped by 60 percent. Livestock prices were not so badly hit, but down they went by nearly 40 percent.

When the excess stocks had been sold, industry could once again look to the future. Excess industrial capacity was put to work. Business revived.

Just as many factors had contributed to the postwar depression, so several changes contributed to the developing boom. The public, for instance, felt more prosperous and began to buy, as unemployment declined and the business outlook improved. Even by 1923, consumer outlays were well above the peak reached in the war boom. Along came installment credit, as we have seen earlier, and millions of Americans rushed out to buy automobiles, clothes, radios, and refrigerators, and to pay for them later.

Manufacturing capacity increased. A boom in residential housing began. New types of metal alloys, new fabrics such as rayon, and rising consumer demand for a very wide variety of goods and entertainment—all helped give industrial growth an extra push.

The automobile industry led the way in mass production. Demand for electricity soared. Only the farmers, among major groups, did not share in the new prosperity.

The ups and downs of the economy could be told at length, but the details are not so important as the main upward trend of economic development and industrial production in the years leading up to 1929. This is perhaps best seen in the history of the automobile industry. Only 4,000 vehicles were produced in 1900, at which time the total number of cars registered in the entire country was only 8,000. In 1920, nearly two million vehicles were made and over eight million were registered. By 1929, the annual output of cars approached the five-million level and total registration amounted to over twenty-three million.

How important this was to the general economy can be gauged by thinking of the steel, glass, rubber, nickel, lead, and other materials that went into the manufacture of those cars. The automobile industry alone gave a great thrust to the entire economy.

The 1920s also saw a great advance in technological progress. Industrial productivity, or output per man-hour, rose as mass production methods spread through much of industry. In fact, output per man-hour in manufacturing industry nearly doubled between 1909 and 1929. By the late 1920s, the theory of standardized interchangeable parts had spread to most sections of industry. Scientific management had helped to cut costs. Mechanical power almost completely replaced animal power (mainly horses). Also, mechanical ingenuity was spurred by the absence of unskilled labor, a state of affairs brought about in part by rising standards of education but mainly by the ending of mass immigration from Europe.

Not surprisingly, an optimistic people felt that prosperity was and should be endless. Why not? The New World was not like the Old. The United States had been successful in conquering the wilderness and had settled three million square miles. She had rescued the old powers of Europe in World War I. And now, after a postwar setback, her economy was booming again and all but the farmers were sitting pretty. Consider, for example, the construction industry, one of the main props of the American economy. In the brief span between 1921 and 1926, construction outlays rose by nearly 80 percent and directly stimulated the demand for all the items that go into building, from lumber and bricks to glass and nails. So why couldn't the economic boom last for ever? Americans thought it would, could, and should.

It was not to be. From time immemorial, droughts have followed extensive floods; the seven fat years have been succeeded by seven lean years. Also, the United States was now very much a world power in every sense of both words. Her development affected all other industrial and trading nations. In turn, she was helped or hindered by trends abroad, especially in Europe.

The major nations of Europe, including Russia (later the Soviet Union), had suffered seriously in the war. Some, such as Russia, had collapsed. Others, such as Germany, experienced such rampant inflation after World War I that money became almost worthless (by the end of 1923, for instance, mailing a letter in Germany cost 100 billion marks).

Much instability existed generally in Europe where the aristocracy of politics, industry, and finance often was badly equipped to run nations that offered little opportunity to most citizens. Yet World War I had vastly im-

proved the social and economic conditions of millions of
Europeans. Class distinctions and caste thinking had been
damaged by the war, even though they still remained as
barriers to highly productive and democratic nations. Europe was still very much a closed society in which many
traces of feudalism could be found. The people were ruled,
rather than governed, even in those countries, such as
Britain, that gave wide voting rights to its people.

Just what part Europe played in the Wall Street collapse of 1929 is debatable, but what went on in Wall Street
was also seen on the London Stock Exchange, the Paris
Bourse, and the stock markets in Germany.

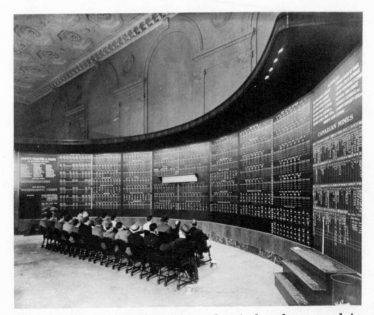

Watching the board. Teleregister electric board was used in
broker's boardrooms from May, 1929. *Courtesy Bunker Ramo.*

Another factor in the stock market collapse, without doubt, was the financial structure of companies in the United States and in Europe. We have seen earlier how many companies issue common stock; that is, shares of ownership in the company. Bonds also are often sold, but these are loans, not part of ownership. This is putting things very simply, since very complex capitalization structures are possible. Also, one company may own much of another company. Building a pyramid among companies is just as possible as the pyramiding mentioned earlier and found in stock market speculation. In short, a vast superstructure of company finance can be built on a very small base.

Just as speculators can increase their profits by borrowing money and buying more securities with the original profits, so companies can grow large with very little capital by employing it effectively in so-called holding companies. Holding companies have long been a favorite form of corporate finance. They are corporations that hold common stock in other companies and thus control or own them even though their common stock investment may be relatively small. Of course, the capital structures of the companies controlled are made to fit such a scheme, and often they are not very sound in relation to total capital. In the heady days of the 1920s, pyramiding by way of holding companies was commonplace. In fact, the Van Sweringen brothers of Cleveland later became so adept at this form of company finance that it became known as the Van Sweringen pyramid.

Several factors, therefore, contributed heavily to the stock market collapse of 1929. One, of course, was the genuine economic prosperity that justified—but only to a certain extent—a rising stock market.

Another factor was the excessive speculation in the stock market that pushed prices far higher than justified even in times of prosperity. Much if not most of this speculation was margin trading; that is, the buying and selling of securities on the payment of a small deposit called a margin. This by itself created market instability, in that even a small change in the price of a stock could wipe out thousands of speculators and bring the price down heavily.

Then there was the top-heavy capital structure of many corporations, which threatened to tumble when the financial weather got rough. Through the holding-company system and pyramiding, many companies could be affected, even toppled, when the narrow company base at the bottom was adversely affected by the market decline or a financial panic.

Other factors included the inside control of the stock market, big business, and finance, and the way insiders could manipulate the stock market by using vast sums to move stocks up and down. One particular form of manipulation used was the process known as selling short, or short sales. A sudden sale of hundreds of thousands of shares will obviously tend to depress the price and frighten genuine holders. If this spate of selling triggers more selling, those that started the panic might well be able to buy back their original stock for less than they sold it for originally. Since they may have borrowed the stock in the first place, these bear raiders, as they are called, would simply repay the loan of the stock and keep the profits.

The bear raid was a fact of financial life in the roaring 1920s. Often enough it worked, but sometimes it did not.

Then, a bear squeeze occurred, and the bears, or short sellers, were hurt, since they could end up paying much more just to get back the stock they had sold earlier at a lower price. Today, short selling is controlled by many rules designed to protect genuine investors.

So the stage had been set for the bull market and collapse. Political instability in Europe, the business boom, the speculation on the world's stock exchanges—all these must have contributed to the final crash.

Yet it is interesting to note that two of the main supports of the economic boom, the automobile industry and the construction industry, had begun to fade even before the stock market went on its final last upsurge in 1928 and 1929. In short, the business props to the stock market boom had weakened.

Not that many people noticed it. All industries rise and fall. They do not grow in a straight line but suffer ups and downs as the years pass. Also, nothing is unusual if a booming industry, or the stock market for that matter, has a bit of a breather to catch a second wind.

Even so, those that are looking for causes of the stock market crash must surely seek basic reasons as well as the technical ones (such as gambling in stocks and the financial structure of corporations). Without doubt, the economic boom was developing weak legs as 1928 yielded to 1929. It is important now to see just how the stock market itself was behaving in that period immediately before the plug was pulled, before stocks fell horribly, and before millions lost much of their capital—and even their shirts.

5. The Great Bull Market

COMPANIES FINANCE THEIR BUSINESS by issuing bonds, which are loans on which interest is paid, and by issuing shares of common stock, which represents part-ownership in the company and on which the companies pay dividends. The interest on bonds has to be paid before any dividends are paid on common stock. Let us say that a company makes a profit of $1 million in a given year. If $1 million has to be paid out as interest to the bondholders, nothing is left for the stockholders. But suppose the company makes $2 million in the following year. Then $1 million will be available to pay to the stockholders. In short, stockholders are last on the profit list, so the amount available to them moves up and down from year to year.

Then again, a company need not pay out big dividends even though a large amount is left after payment of interest to the bondholders. The company may decide to pay either small dividends or large dividends; it may decide to

42

reinvest all, some, or none of its profits in business expansion.

Also, long-term business booms come along, and these often are followed by long business slumps. During these ups and downs of the business cycle, the bondholders are entitled to the same amount, but, as we have seen above, the amount available for stockholders may change sharply, even from year to year. So, in a real boom, the stockholders may do very well indeed. Their dividends may actually rise by several hundred percent within a few years.

Investors, being both anxious and ambitious, want to keep their capital intact and also make a lot more. They do not care to be left out of a good thing, since this also reflects on their investment ability. So they tend to rush in and buy stocks when others are buying; a popular stock attracts much attention. Similarly, in times of panic, they rush to sell, often without even thinking what they are doing.

It is clear from this that stock prices must move much more violently than business activity does. They always have done so and still do. In fact, business itself is not able to grow very quickly. It takes time to build factories and train workers. Much capital is needed. Corporate prosperity is not built overnight.

We have seen how certain industries, such as automobiles, radios, and construction, moved ahead very quickly after World War I. But the resources made available for these industries were obviously not available to other industries. The growth in total industrial output during the years leading up to the stock market crash in 1929 was nowhere near so great as the boom in stock prices. For instance, the value of manufacturing output rose by only

12 percent between 1925 and 1929. Total industrial production rose by only 90 percent between 1921 and 1929. That is less than 10 percent per year, compounded.

Even so, such growth may reasonably be regarded as representing good business conditions, albeit ones that are unlikely to last forever. Business earnings naturally rose. The net amount available for stockholders, after paying interest to bondholders, rose much faster. Consequently, bigger dividends were paid. Investors felt wealthy, since their stocks were going up, they were receiving larger dividends, and the economic outlook was rosy.

Many people who normally bought securities as investments for income decided to take a turn at stock speculation, usually defined as buying securities with the hope of selling fairly quickly at a profit. Sometimes, speculators bought risky stocks on the stock market. At other times, they went outside the stock market and bought real estate, as in Florida. But when the Florida real estate boom began to fade in 1926, these plungers became more interested again in speculating on the stock market.

This influx of speculators tended to push up the prices of stocks. Stock prices, of course, always move up and down for many economic, financial, and psychological reasons. But the higher they go, the faster they fall when the speculative tide begins to ebb. Until 1926, stock prices were not unreasonably high in relation to business earnings. Investors were receiving good dividends, and the yield on their investments was quite generous. As more and more people became convinced that prosperity was here to stay, stock prices rose further. From time to time, there were the usual setbacks, but, that being normal in the stock market, little attention was paid to them.

The year 1924, for instance, was a good one for the stock market. So was 1925. Between May 1924 and December 1925, stock prices rose 70 percent on average. That is certainly a good gain.

A setback followed early in 1926. A business decline discouraged investors, and stock prices fell sharply in February and March of that year. By March, stock prices were only one third higher than they had been two years earlier. This setback proved only temporary, and investors began to turn in droves from Florida real estate to the stock market. Stock prices advanced. By 1927, a real bull market in stocks was under way.

The position is clearly seen by comparing stock price levels at the end of each year. Between 1925 and 1926, for instance, stock prices had actually fallen fractionally, but, between December 1926 and December 1927, they rose by about 40 percent on average, even though setbacks had occurred in between.

So it may be said that 1925 saw the real beginnings of the bull market, that 1926 was a year when prices were consolidated, that 1927 prepared the way for the sharp advance in 1928, and that 1929 was the year of the hysterical boom and gigantic collapse.

Investors, of course, do not buy the market averages or the various indices of stock price movements. An average is simply an average price of a number of stocks. An index is the same sort of thing but expressed in percentage terms. Although these averages and indices are needed to measure and show what stock prices are doing, in general, they are not a clear indication of how a particular investor is faring or of what he should do. If, for example, the stock market goes up by 50 percent on average, one stock may have risen

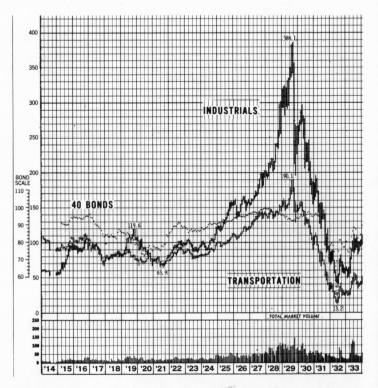

The Dow Jones Averages for the period 1914–33 show the ups and downs of the average prices of selected bonds, industrial stocks, and transportation stocks. The bars at the bottom show the volume of shares (in millions) on the New York Stock Exchange.

by 200 percent, another by 100 percent, and yet another by 50 percent. And other stocks may not have changed in value while still others may have fallen. That is why so many investors today are often disillusioned over market averages. They may see their own stocks falling while the market averages rise.

A similar state of affairs applied in the great bull market that ended in 1929. It was indeed a bull market, but the idea that all stocks and bonds soared to great heights in 1929 is quite false. Some stocks were favorites. Others were dogs, to use the market expression.

It is useful for us to look at the average price of stocks during the great bull market. The year 1926 was one of consolidation in the stock market, since prices at the end of the year were just about what they were at the beginning. Taking 1926 as the base year, therefore, we find that stock prices had just about doubled by the time the stock market peaked in 1929.

That is a good gain and very acceptable to most investors, but there is nothing really exceptional about it.

What is more, such a gain was justified—at least to some extent. Stock prices are supposed to reflect economic prosperity, and there was indeed economic prosperity; higher stock prices tended to be solidly based on company earnings and prospects. The trend of stock prices is supposed to show the confidence that investors have in their country, and Americans were supremely confident that good times had come to stay. So a rising stock market was justified.

Just how much higher stock prices should have been on a rational basis is not easy to gauge, in that the stock market reflects hopes and fears as well as a cool appraisal of current prospects.

It may even be argued that stock prices were too high in 1926, and that the doubling of prices between 1926 and 1929 simply made a bad case worse. This argument has some merit. In fact, the boom in stock prices between May

1924 and December 1925 compares very favorably with that following 1926 and leading up to 1929. In December 1926, though, stock prices were not so high that a slump in Wall Street would have triggered a gigantic collapse of the economy and helped develop a worldwide economic depression.

Between June 1928 and June 1929, stock prices rose by less than one third on average. So while the high level of stock prices certainly played a role in the events of 1929 and later, it was not by any means the only factor in the collapse. The basic factor without doubt was the speculative mania that not only pushed prices high but operated on very little margin—that is, some stocks worth a small fortune on paper were bought for only a few thousand dollars put down as a deposit; but when prices collapsed, the deposit was quickly lost unless the speculator was able to add to the deposit.

In the 1920s, the Federal Reserve Board did not have the power, as it now does, to fix margin (deposit) requirements. This was left to the brokers. Many brokers insisted that their customers put down a sizable deposit when buying securities. This had grown to 50 percent of the cost in many cases by 1929. However, each broker pleased himself, and, being anxious to get the business and commissions, was usually generous. He himself, of course, could borrow money on the security of the stocks bought.

There is not very much merit to the view that, in the 1929 bull market, certain stocks were market favorites and that when they collapsed they brought the whole market down with them.

Nor was the volume of trading (often regarded as an indicator of speculative enthusiasm) on the New York

Stock Exchange up to 1928 and 1929 particularly heavy compared with that in later years. The volume did rise sharply, of course, growing by over half between 1927 and 1928.

Speculators could actually see their money grow enormously or disappear before their eyes as they watched the ticker tape. Between April 1926 and September 1929, industrial stock prices in general more than doubled, while numerous popular securities rose by several hundred percent.

Sharp declines would follow a boom, and sharp rallies came after setbacks. Daily moves of five points (dollars) became commonplace in the more popular and the more speculative securities. As speculation increased, certain stocks began bobbing about like corks in an angry sea. These included United States Steel (known simply as Steel), Radio Corporation of America (known as Radio), General Electric, General Motors, Montgomery Ward, Westinghouse, and many, many more.

Trading, of course, took place all over the country, since investors usually give their orders to buy and sell securities to their local broker. New York City got most of the attention, since that is the site of the New York Stock Exchange, and that exchange, then and now, is the premier stock exchange. The smaller exchanges in other cities usually base their prices of securities on those being quoted in New York.

In this feverish frenzy, almost anything could happen, even though interest rates on money borrowed for stock market speculation were high, and the supply of credit was not large by earlier standards—despite higher savings from economic prosperity.

The ups and downs of the stock market, as had occurred in years such as 1925 and 1926, were magnified greatly in 1927, 1928, and 1929. By 1928, stock prices were clearly unstable; the normal daily changes in stock prices of $1 or $2 grew as the months passed. By the time the great bull market reached its peak in 1929, changes of $5 and $10 were common in the most popular stocks. When the stock market crashed, a decline of $10 in one day was nothing, and daily swings of $30 or more were seen in market favorites such as General Electric and Montgomery Ward.

The stock market was in turmoil during those hectic years of boom and collapse. The ticker machine was running so late, because of heavy sales, that no one could find out what stocks were actually selling for. Pandemonium reigned even on the New York Stock Exchange's trading floor.

A stock market suddenly full of speculators that have been cleaned out is not an optimistic place. It takes time, of course, to end a rampant bull market since, although it looks dead, it often will not lie down quietly—if only because hope springs eternal in the speculator's breast. As it was, spirit and optimism still existed in Wall Street long after the initial crash in 1929. Not many people expected the economy to follow the example of the stock market. But it did, and by so doing it pushed the stock market down and down and down.

6. Finding the Scapegoat

THE PAROXYSMS THAT BEGAN to shake Wall Street in 1928 had their counterpart abroad. The idea that only the American people had taken leave of their senses, and that the rest of the world was sane and calm, should be resisted. But only a brief account of conditions abroad can be given here.

World War I had caused massive social change in Europe, but the old ways of international finance were not quickly forgotten by those accustomed to the serenity of the years before 1914.

The keystone in those days was gold. World trade was on the gold standard. We have seen earlier how Britain abandoned the gold standard, temporarily at least, in 1914. Gold was then too valuable to be used as currency, or freely exchanged for foreign monies. Britain's gold stocks were needed to fight the war and feed the people, since so much of Britain's food was imported.

After the war, some Britons urged a return to the gold standard, despite the changed conditions of domestic and international finance. They believed, as some people still

51

do, that gold, a valuable metal, provides a solid backing for a paper currency when that paper currency may be freely exchanged for gold. So in 1925, Britain returned to the gold standard. It was not the same gold standard that prevailed up to 1914, but a different variety known as the gold exchange standard. Under this system, gold was not used as part of the nation's currency, but only as a means to settle international debts, such as those resulting from trade. So the pound sterling was linked to gold at the pre-war rate of $4.867 to the pound sterling. This simply means that the pound sterling, in terms of its value in gold, was worth the same as $4.867, in terms of gold. The world's major currencies, that is the paper money similar to that used today, each had a specific value in terms of so much gold.

This step had two serious consequences. The pound was overvalued in terms of other currencies, which meant that foreigners had to pay too high a price in their own currencies to get British currency with which to buy British goods. In short, the pound was simply not worth the price. British goods were expensive to foreigners, who tended, naturally, to buy elsewhere. Also, Britain had to be careful about printing too much paper currency, lest foreign nations lose confidence in Britain's ability to convert her foreign trade debts, on demand, into gold at the fixed rate. That was the basic meaning of being on the gold standard. In the same way, Britain's unwillingness to print adequate paper money tended to restrict her industrial development and hurt trade.

British goods, such as textiles and coal, suffered seriously in the traditional export markets since they were expensive to foreign buyers. Attempts to reduce costs at home, by keeping wages down, brought on a general strike over most of the nation in 1926.

The situation in Germany was not much better. Germany had been shattered in World War I and her currency had to be later abandoned when it became almost worthless because of uncontrolled inflation. Also, the Treaty of Versailles, which ended World War I, left deep-seated resentment among Germans, partly because the reparations were severe and partly because the territorial settlement was regarded as unfair.

In France, the carnage of World War I shook political life and brought on an instability that was to plague that nation for several decades. Elsewhere in Europe, inflation flourished, vast social changes occurred, and the seeds of much future trouble took deep root.

Not unnaturally, some of the former Allies, such as Britain and France, turned to the United States for assistance. Their mission, in part, was to persuade the Federal Reserve Board, which played a major role in controlling U.S. banking, credit, and the money supply, to make some effort to cut U.S. interest rates and so make the United States a comparatively unattractive place in which to invest. For instance, the Federal Reserve Board, by increasing the money supply at home, could stimulate inflation and make American goods comparatively costly and foreign goods comparatively cheap. By the same token, Americans would be encouraged to invest money in Europe. The Allies were not very successful. By and large, the United States and the major nations in Europe went each its own way. There thus came into being the American myth that, if only the Federal Reserve Board had cooperated with Europe immediately after World War I, no speculative boom would have occurred, no 1929 crash would have developed, and no Depression would have followed. At best, this is a debatable point, but when there is trouble at home, as there also was in many European nations during the 1920s and after, it is easier to blame foreign devils (especially those in Europe), while the Federal Reserve Board, being outside the private sector of the economy, served as the domestic scapegoat.

Foreign nations, of course, also were in deep economic, financial and political trouble. They too found it more convenient to blame scapegoats than to tackle seriously a problem that demanded courage, innovation and massive changes in the structure of business, finance and society. In Europe, dictators began their quest for power, communists were said to be under every bed, most politicians were inept, and unemployment rose.

But the idea that the Federal Reserve banking system, set up under the Federal Reserve Act of 1913, plus a few foreign devils, can be blamed for the stock market speculation and 1929 crash hardly accords with the facts.

Even today, the control of the economy via the decisions of the Federal Reserve Board, is not easy. One reason is psychology. Providing money, or limiting money, is fairly simple, but money is only one aspect of business prosperity and stock market speculation. Businessmen will not borrow money, no matter how low interest rates are, if they do not think the business climate is suitable for expansion. Likewise, speculators will not borrow to buy securities if they are unhappy about the economic outlook. The security of their capital is far more important than low interest rates.

Another allegation is worth examination. This is that

the stock speculation was imported from the stock exchanges of Europe, which had long been accustomed to gambling in securities. No merit attaches to this, however, since the United States had already proved only too conclusively—by such events as the California Gold Rush and the Florida real estate boom—that the urge to get rich quickly is not limited to Europe.

Another factor in the general discussion of responsibility for the 1929 crash is the great size of the United States' economy compared with those of European countries. Clearly, the United States, then as today, dominates world trade and has much the greatest influence in international finance. Other nations, of course, make their own impact, but the giant is the United States. When she trembles, the rest of the world shakes.

The general adoption of the gold exchange standard, the social instability in Germany, and the political instability in France—all contributed to the international financial and trade tensions that grew in the 1920s. But the major responsibility for events in the United States has to be accepted by the American people and institutions. So it was that conditions in the United States during the 1920s reflected the freewheeling financial structure of Wall Street and the nation, the belief that the federal government should keep its hands off big business and finance, and the genuine growth in the American economy that helped generate an orgy of speculation in securities.

The U.S. government, of course, had its own share of responsibility. To give just one example, its independent agency, the Federal Reserve Board, can vary its policies as national and international economic and monetary conditions change. At times, international considerations were the decisive factor in Federal Reserve Board policies. Later, national trends, such as the vast growth in the economy and the development of speculative enthusiasm in the stock market, became far more important than international trade and finance, so far as Federal Reserve Board's banking and credit policies were concerned.

The Federal Reserve Board used banking regulations and changes in its own loan rate to restrict inflation yet keep the economy moving. An easy, or cheap, money policy was more or less followed by the Federal Reserve in the early days of the bull market, when business needed money for expansion. (This was reasonable enough, especially as the Federal Reserve had been blamed, with some justice, for the deflation and slump of 1920–21.) No doubt, international considerations later encouraged the Federal Reserve to maintain a cheap money policy when tighter money at home may have restricted stock speculation but at the expense of a business downturn. Later, the Federal Reserve Board raised interest rates, thus making more expensive the cost of borrowing money for speculation. But, by this time, the stock market boom was well under way.

Today, we see more clearly how difficult it is for the Federal Reserve Board to act truly independently when under so much business and political pressure. In those days, when government interference in business and finance was hotly resented, the unwillingness of the Federal Reserve to be responsible for halting business prosperity and a stock market boom was understandable.

The nation's economy and conditions in Wall Street were also affected by the attitude of business leaders, financiers, and politicians.

Businessmen, of course, were thoroughly opposed to the

idea of monetary regulation through the Federal Reserve system. J. P. Morgan & Company's major importance as a *central* bank for the nation had been ended by the Federal Reserve Act of 1913 (which had created the Federal Reserve banking system) and by the growth of large business corporations able to deal directly with the investing public and with huge corporate funds of their own. But Morgan was still a force in the land for private ownership and control of the banking mechanism. So were other banking firms. They all believed that the government had little or no role to play in Wall Street—or in business, for that matter.

President Calvin Coolidge in the White House was not the sort of person to actively intervene when the economy was booming and stock prices were rising. He was optimistic to the last, and quite justifiably so since the nation was happy and prosperous when he left the White House in March 1929.

Nor was his successor, President Herbert Hoover, to blame for the stock market crash. The final upheaval was under way when Hoover entered the White House, and we see now how the convulsions of 1928 presaged what was later to occur in 1929. Hoover could not have prevented the débâcle. Indeed, many political, business, and financial leaders believed that the stock market would stage an early comeback from the crash.

The stock market has slumped on many occasions since 1929. In many instances, the declines have been severe, despite the much greater restrictions on speculation now in force, to say nothing of the experience remembered from 1929. Booms still occur on the stock exchange, and collapses follow booms. So as we look back to the collapse in 1929, it is wiser not to find scapegoats, or even to try to.

Rather it is best to understand human nature and its willingness to gamble and speculate, as in the South Sea Bubble, the Florida real estate boom, the stock market orgy of 1927 to 1929, and the more recent yet equally fantastic booms that have occurred in specialized stock market groups and securities.

For, like the alchemists of old, many people in many lands wish to turn their lead into gold.

7. The Financial Pot Boils Over

THE YEAR 1928 was the best year, and the last enjoyable full year in that heady, carefree era. By this time, speculation and gambling in the stock market were common.

The financial morals of the time were lax, to say the least. Americans of great repute and social standing thought nothing of participating in pools, the objects of which was to defraud the public in a way that now would be considered indictable. Quite often members of the New York Stock Exchange actually operated some of the pools, the functions of which were to manipulate stocks, attract public attention, and then sell out after widespread buying had forced up the prices. Speculation, in fact, was regarded as highly beneficial to the economy, and was likened to the risk taken when Columbus discovered America.

Stock prices as measured by the market averages and indices showed fantastic fluctuations, but these were nothing compared with the wild gyrations that shook individual securities that had the public's attention.

The situation was not basically affected by the change-over in administrations in March 1929, from that of President Coolidge to that of President Hoover.

During the two years, 1928 and 1929, the nation was almost financially rudderless. Lack of effective action from the White House, and the belief that the Federal Reserve Board would not have the temerity to act decisively to control speculation, encouraged many people to take a flyer in the market.

Stock prices boiled and churned. Nervousness on the part of investors, speculators, and gamblers produced market instability. By the spring of 1928, the point of no return had been reached. A severe shakeout, or a market collapse, had become inevitable. Even so, nothing indicated that a full-fledged business depression was in the offing. The stock market had fallen on many earlier occasions. Little alarm was felt, even though, by all normal standards, the stock market had become a place of extreme risk where many popular stocks were clearly overvalued in terms of any reasonable estimate of earnings and dividends.

The enormous public demand for common stocks was used by many companies to expand and obtain capital while the going was good. It is, of course, advantageous to companies to float new securities when stock prices are high, because fewer new securities will bring in the capital required.

Yet even this spate of new stock issues, as they are called, failed to calm the market. The public, in fact, was stimulated by visions of a new society and a bright future. Radios, automobiles, chain stores, banks, utilities, theaters, and holding companies were among the many groups to enjoy public enthusiasm.

Investors also were intrigued with two ideas that promised even bigger company profits and better opportunities in the stock market. Mergers attracted attention in a day when managerial ability commanded a huge premium. Investment trusts enjoyed a fantastic promotion, even though they simply enabled investors to take an interest in many securities by buying just one. These trusts, of course, had to buy in the market the stocks for their portfolios (the name given to the list of securities held by an investor or financial house). In this way, countless investors were deluded into thinking they had real financial security just because their risk was spread among many stocks. The buying of a wide variety of stocks in the market by these investment trusts helped spread the view that all industries and all stocks would participate in the new era of endless prosperity.

By June of 1928, the gyrations in Wall Street had become convulsive. The old days when one million shares were traded had given way to three-million-share days, then four- and five-million-share days. Prices of individual securities rose and fell by ten or twenty points (dollars) a day. Brokerage offices were crowded.

By November, heavy buying put the daily volume at more than six million shares—a new record. More and more Americans were speculating in the market, often by putting down a small margin in a brokerage house. Many of these purchases were made "at the market"—that is, at the going price no matter what it is. This form of order to buy, as distinguished from buying at a fixed price, became necessary when hectic trading made the current price unavailable. Investors were so anxious to get onto a good thing, before the price went higher, that they could not wait for a more up-to-date price than that quoted on the ticker tape, which often was hours late. In short, the tape recording the transactions was showing what the price was, say, two hours earlier. Anything could have happened since. Many investors found they had bought at prices much higher than expected and at many points higher than the subsequent closing price that day. Their purchases started off to a loss.

The picture painted is one of chaos, but, during the course of 1928, industrial stocks as a whole rose by only one third. As is usual, however, individual stocks, especially those with popular support, rose much more sharply. The advent of radio, for instance, had made the Radio Corporation of America a popular speculative vehicle. The stock rose by some 400 percent in 1928.

The fever of 1928 reached its crisis in 1929. The violent speculation in Wall Street during 1928 had caused such price booms and setbacks that the end of the great bull market had seemed near to many investors.

It was not to be. The boom continued with even greater vigor in 1929. By this time, money rates in Wall Street were high, but these attracted loans from far and wide, and speculators borrowed at high rates expecting to make a killing in stocks. What was 10 or 15 percent *a year* in interest when popular stocks doubled in price within a few months? The argument was justified in part, in that many stocks did precisely that. This applied both to stocks of first rank, which were usually high in price, and to inferior securities, which sold for only a few dollars and consequently were bought with greater enthusiasm by those investors who felt they were getting a lot for their money. Many of the very popular issues among big investors, such as Radio, U. S. Steel, Du Pont, and General Electric, traded at several hundred dollars per share. Thousands of other stocks, however, sold for much less, although of course, the price rose greatly as the stock boom continued.

Herbert Hoover, who had recently taken office as President, proved incapable of taking effective action to control speculation. Nor could he have been anxious to make any move that might also have put an end to the general business prosperity. Both the U.S. Treasury and the Federal Reserve Board felt it wiser not to intervene too actively, if at all.

So the great bull market lurched on. Its spasms during 1929 attracted increasing attention at home and abroad, but otherwise the nation was placid and fairly content. Most people went about their business in the usual way. Those interested in the stock market were naturally excited as one stock after another was given a run-up by insiders, manipulators, or pools.

Almost unknown to most Americans was the declining output of two of the nation's most vital industries—automobile manufacture and construction. Neither setback was major. Both industries had boomed for years, and a modest decline in their level of business activity was only to be expected. Even so, the combination was such that some of the steam was taken out of the economic boom. This, in turn, had an impact on the stock market, because many investors had been buying stocks on the assumption that rising business prosperity would continue. Now, a slight change had occurred.

The business boom had lost some of its bloom. The stock market was clearly boiling over. A few, but only a few, Americans decided to sell their securities in order to make a profit. The rest simply could not believe the great bull market was all over.

8. After the Bull Was Over

No BELL IS TOLLED when a bull market dies. On September 3, 1929, few investors were aware of its passing. Small wonder, since prices had been gyrating for eighteen months, with automobile stocks, radio stocks, and aviation stocks being among the favorites in the last mad surge. September 3 was just another day of ups and downs in the market.

But it was a boom with ebbing industrial support. For over a year, many businessmen had been aware that the economy was not so buoyant as many people thought. They also were aware that stock prices had soared to such heights that even a very optimistic industrial future had been discounted, or allowed for. But the bull market psychology was there. The money was available. All the talk of an economic setback was ignored by speculators who went on a wild buying spree.

When business fails to move ahead, when company profits are not good, a great amount of hot air from speculative enthusiasm is needed to support a top-heavy stock market. Sooner or later, though, such optimism must be supported by reality or it will disappear. Stock prices cannot remain high indefinitely, propped up merely by speculative demand.

The final burst of the speculative mania came early in September, when a rapid cooling of the feverish atmosphere was quickly felt as better quality stocks began to lose several points a day. Some of them soon had lost more than fifty points. U.S. Steel, General Electric, Radio Corporation of America, and dozens of others were down sharply.

Yet the market rallied. Sharp breaks had been seen before in Wall Street. Many speculators, accustomed to buying on declines, simply stepped in. This time, however, no major boom came to carry stock prices to new highs.

By mid-October, the stock market was in a bad way. Pessimism and fear replaced optimism and greed. Great waves of selling shook the market. Reputable brokers began asking their customers to pay more margin; that is, to pay more cash into their accounts to make up for the sharp decline in the value of their stocks that had not been paid for in full. Many investors could not oblige. So their stocks were sold. That helped push stock prices lower. This frightened other speculators, who also sold. Rumors were heard that support would be forthcoming from banks, investment trusts, members of the stock exchange, and big operators in the stock market, who, it was said and hoped, could not afford to see the market collapse. But the big operators were themselves in trouble because of the sharp declines that had occurred in the prices of many high quality stocks. The impression that no help would be forthcoming from the big operators was confirmed on October

October 25, 1929: The bull market had ended in September, 1929, but the real crash started in October. © 1929 by The New York Times Company. Reprinted by permission.

London *Times* for October 25, 1929. The Wall Street panic was a major news story in Britain. *Courtesy London* Times.

24—a day that later came to be called Black Thursday—
when stock prices broke decisively. So few investors were
willing to buy that, often enough, stocks were sold almost
literally for anything they would bring.

That same afternoon, however, some bankers did move
in, buying here and there and restoring, for a time at least,
some of the former optimism. Indeed, many investors
thought the worst was over—that the market would turn up
again as it had done after a similar skid in 1928.

It was not to be. Too many investors, speculators, and
gamblers must have been counting their winnings and losses
on Sunday, October 27, for, on Monday, the market was
deluged with selling orders. Panic was widespread.

Part of this came from the investors' inability to discover
what was happening on the New York Stock Exchange.
Normally, of course, the stock ticker tape provided a very
clear idea of prices and at what prices stocks could be sold
and bought for if an order were to be given. But, on days
of heavy volume, the ticker ran late, often hours late. An
investor looking at the tape in his broker's office could
easily read the current prices at which the favorite stocks
had been traded because they appeared on the tape frequently. But when the ticker was late, the prices given were
the prices that had been made on sales two or more hours
earlier. Even that delay was not too harmful when stock
prices fluctuated by only a few points in a day. But when
panic prevailed, and stocks fell by ten, twenty, or thirty
points or more in a day, the delay in the tape's prices could
be disastrous.

So it was that, on Monday, October 28, real fear and
panic swept over brokerage houses and investors. Those
people who had bought stocks on margin found themselves

not only wiped out completely but owing money as well. Millions of shares were thrown onto the market in desperation, as investors found themselves facing bankruptcy.

This time, the big bankers were missing. They themselves had problems. Many of their investments had fallen more in a few days than they had gained in the preceding twelve months. The money that earlier had flooded Wall Street, to take advantage of high interest rates and the stock market boom, suddenly left for greener and presumably safer pastures. Some banks actually did step in and help out with loans, thus shielding the stock market from even more panic selling to get money to repay earlier loans made by brokers to stock buyers, and which the lenders now called, that is asked the borrower to repay.

October proved cruel to investors. Prices had crashed. The bull market was over. The victims wandered the streets almost too stunned to know what had happened.

But life carried on. Buying and selling continued on the New York Stock Exchange as elsewhere. Rallies came along, followed by further slumps. Indeed, had the stock market crash of 1929 completed its work by the end of October, the boom would be known simply as a mania that ran its course in less than two years.

It was far more than that. The great bull market had not been built entirely on delusions. Up to March 1928, stock prices and the economy had marched hand in hand, with stock prices gradually exaggerating the growth in industrial output and company profits. Stock prices had also represented the confidence of the American people in their country. This too was justified, in that the United States had emerged from World War I as the financial and business leader of the world.

When stock prices broke, people felt betrayed. They had put their trust in a system that failed them simply because the stock market moves to excess. The great era of confidence was over. Bankers and businessmen were shaken, as well as small investors. A drawing in of horns was the natural result of Wall Street losses amounting to billions of dollars.

Companies needing capital found it harder to float new issues of stocks. Business suffered. Banks had huge losses on their investment portfolios; they were also forced to cut back on loans. Investment trusts had been routed because they merely held securities, which had dropped like the rest. Holding companies were shaken since the pyramided structure of many of them was weakened by investment losses, lower stock prices, and the calling in of bank loans.

What few people recognized in October 1929 was the emergence of a new era, in which falling stock prices would drag the economy down, year after year, just as a rising stock market had earlier helped business expansion. The two, of course, fuel each other, with stock prices usually leading the way both up and down. Industrial prosperity normally brings a booming stock market, which, in turn, helps industry expand by providing capital funds for expansion. On the way down, a falling stock market either helps trigger a business recession or makes worse an existing economic decline.

The enormous losses suffered in the stock market break of September–October 1929 were by themselves enough to bring on a business setback even if the economy had been prosperous. As it was, business was already suffering a decline, and it got a decisive shove downward from the stock market collapse. Not that all this occurred overnight.

The stock market boom had taken years to develop. The stock market collapse took years to run its course.

The business setback also gradually deepened as the years passed. It became the Great Depression. In turn, the Depression ushered in a new world of federal government intervention in monetary and stock exchange matters. Central authorities took on wide responsibility for the well-being of the people. Today, the stock market crash of 1929 is looked upon as the end of the era of laissez-faire. In the succeeding era, the freedom to gamble and speculate was controlled; laws were passed to protect investors; the stock exchanges ceased to be privileged places where members of private clubs could legally cheat investors; banks were regulated; and holding companies and investment trusts came under government scrutiny.

It took time—several years in fact—before the new order came into being, under a new President, Franklin D. Roosevelt. Not that President Hoover could be blamed for the stock market crash, but his thoughts were attuned to the old belief that industry and finance should be left alone and that, if they were, the people would fare well.

The people fared badly, though. The efforts made by President Hoover to help the economy were basically unsuccessful, because they did not measure up to what was needed—namely a new philosophy of some measure of public control over all those aspects of life that provide the public's well-being.

9. The Extent of the Damage

THE CRASH THAT WAS HEARD around the world in October 1929 echoed and re-echoed throughout the nation and humanity, bringing in its wake a vast tide of churning emotions as the stock market dropped, recovered for a few months in late 1929 and early 1930, then began the plunge that for two years brought personal disaster to millions and an economic depression that will live forever in memory.

The extent of the stock market decline by itself is almost unbelievable. Even in 1929 alone, two or three months of falling prices erased the gains of two years and some $30 billion. But this was nothing compared with what followed.

A variety of statistics exists on this subject, but they all tell the same tale: the carnage was a national disaster. Between the high-water mark of 1929 and the low tide of 1932, for instance, the prices of industrial stocks fell by over 85 percent. Railroad securities dropped by over 90 percent. On the New York Stock Exchange, the amount of stock trading between 1929 and 1932 fell by over 60 percent; in 1934, it was less than 30 percent of that in 1929.

A similarly grim record is shown by the number of

bankruptcies. In September 1929, the month before the crash, there were over 1,500 business failures—the usual monthly figure. But in January 1932, there were nearly 3,500. (By September 1934, though, the number was down to less than 800, since few new firms were being formed.)

The sickening crunch of financial losses was seen in the net profits of corporations; such profits declined by over 75 percent between 1929 and 1932. Some industries, of course, fared worse than others. Industrial and commercial companies actually reported a deficit in 1932 after being cock-of-the-walk in 1929. So did the manufacturers of automobiles, steel and railroad equipment, metals, and machinery, and mining companies. Important railroads were not so badly hit. Their profits fell by about 75 percent between 1929 and 1932. That was a lot better than the record of the once-proud automobile companies, which hit the financial skids far faster than their autos had ever hit the road.

One stout group was the utilities. Their profits fell by only one third. This included the telephone companies. Apparently, people were talking as much as usual, even though they were enjoying life less. Certainly, they had plenty to talk about.

Naturally enough, in times such as these, few companies went to Wall Street to raise capital. Between 1929 and 1933, the total dollar volume of new capital issues fell by over 90 percent. In 1927, a record 265 foreign capital issues were publicly offered in the United States; only two were so offered in 1934.

Wholesale prices and retail food prices fell by about 40 percent. Farm prices dropped by over 60 percent.

By the spring of 1933, over four million families were on

"All the News That's Fit to Print."

The New York Times.

THE WEATHER

VOL. LXXIX...No. 26,211.   NEW YORK, TUESDAY, OCTOBER 29, 1929.   TWO CENTS

BINGHAM ACCUSES SENATORS OF PLOT TO BESMIRCH HIM; NORRIS TO ASK FOR CENSURE

BINGHAM'S ATTACK BITTER

Charges Lobby Inquiry With Throwing at Him 'Political Slime.'

CALLS ITS METHODS UNFAIR

Caraway Asking These to Stand Who Approve Espinosa Episode, Gets No Response.

OTHER MEMBERS NOT BACK

Norris Will Draw Up Resolution Against Connecticut Senator for Presentation Today.

SENATORS RENEW DEMAND ON HOOVER FOR TARIFF STAND

Johnson and Harrison Call for His Guidance as Chamber Clashes Over Bill's Fate.

CONFERENCE DEMISE SEEN

Accusing Republicans of This Aim, Simmons Holds President Responsible With Party.

SMOOT ISSUES CHALLENGE

KAROLYIS GET RIGHT TO ENTER COUNTRY

Stimson Raises Ban Against Hungarian Count and Countess Placed by Hughes in 1925.

LIBERAL POLICY IS SEEN

Secretary, Granting Visa, Says Department to Pass Albert on Different Set of Rules.

Roosevelt's Memory Honored in Navy Day Fete as Ships

EUROPE IS DISTURBED BY AMERICAN ACTION ON OCCUPATION DEBT

London Urges an Explanation of Move to Direct Payments by Germany.

BANK'S PRESTIGE INVOLVED

Britain and Continent Feel That We Do Not Have Faith in Young Plan Institution.

SCHEME IS LAID TO HOOVER

SENATOR T. E. BURTON LONG ILL, DIES AT 77

Ohio Statesman Had Served in Congress for 41 Years—First Elected to the House.

STRONG ADVOCATE OF PEACE

STOCK PRICES SLUMP $14,000,000,000 IN NATION-WIDE STAMPEDE TO UNLOAD; BANKERS TO SUPPORT MARKET TODAY

Sixteen Leading Issues Down $2,893,520,108; Tel. & Tel. and Steel Among Heaviest Losers

PREMIER ISSUES HARD HIT

Unexpected Torrent of Liquidation Again Rocks Markets.

DAY'S SALES 9,212,800

Nearly 3,000,000 Shares Are Traded in Final Hour—The Tickers Lag 167 Minutes.

NEW RALLY SOON BROKEN

AIRLINER IS LOST WITH 5 IN STORM

Last Reported Heading for New Mexico Region When the T. A. T. Plane Crashed.

SEEN NEAR MOUNT TAYLOR

BANKERS MOBILIZE FOR BUYING TODAY

Well St. Is Certain Coalition Has Decided to Throw Funds Into Market for Support.

INVESTMENT TRUSTS TO AID

City Traffic Lights Now Blink 20 Hours a Day; Whalen Also Cuts Intervals to Speed Vehicles

Architects Picked to Plan Rockefeller Centre, Which May Have Opera House as a Nucleus

---

October 29, 1929: One wave of selling followed another. Stocks continued to tumble. © 1929 by The New York Times Company. Reprinted by permission.

74

STOCKS COLLAPSE IN 16,410,030-SHARE DAY, BUT RALLY AT CLOSE CHEERS BROKERS; BANKERS OPTIMISTIC, TO CONTINUE AID

October 30, 1929: Finally, stock prices simply collapsed under weight of selling, often panic selling at whatever prices the stocks would bring. © 1929 by The New York Times Company. Reprinted by permission.

unemployment relief, the average relief benefits per family being about $15 monthly. Small wonder that few automobiles were being sold!

The extent of the calamity boggles the imagination. Why could people not see what was happening? That's a natural question to ask. It has been asked before in history, and will be asked again. The answer, of course, is that people could clearly see and feel what was happening.

Crowd at Wall Street in front of the Bank of New York during the panic due to heavy stock trading, October, 1929. *Courtesy U.S. Information Agency.*

But there existed no national scheme to cope with such a financial and economic disaster. The old laissez-faire attitude prevailed.

Nor was there much international cooperation. In Britain, investment confidence on the London Stock Exchange had been hard hit by the dishonest financing methods of a man named Clarence Hatry, whose financial empire had collapsed in 1929. Developments on the continent of Europe did nothing to help matters. The fact that Britain was on the gold exchange standard, until a depression was too late to avert, is a tribute to the power that gold had, and still has, over some of the otherwise most perceptive minds. France, of course, was already beginning to show that fatal weakness in leadership that led to her defeat and occupation by Germany in just about a decade. In Germany, the man who later became infamous as Hitler was already on the march to power. Big German and Austrian banks saw their money disappearing as foreign depositors decided that democracy in Germany would not be working much longer.

Attempts at home and abroad were made to shore up the U.S. economy and get industry moving again. Rallies occurred now and again. Hope revived, then was dashed, as unemployment rose painfully to around thirteen million (to use an average of the various unofficial estimates).

Soup kitchens fed many who were hungry. Some men sold apples while others panhandled. People fished in and fought for garbage.

The well-to-do children that went to college came out to face a world bleak with disappointment and chilled with despair.

Not all Americans were out of work. Those that were fully employed were comparatively very well off, in that the cost of living was low. This deflation helped those that had fixed incomes, such as interest from government securities. Even in the Depression, some gained, but many lost.

The tragedy lay in blighted lives for tens of millions, in suffering and poverty. The nation was disillusioned—not only by the stock market collapse, by the Depression that grew in intensity almost every day, and by the feeling of hopelessness and despair among millions of Americans who wished only to work, but also by what was revealed by the financial failure of banks, stock brokerage houses, and industrial companies. Even by the low ethical standards of those days, many respected Americans were found to have been corrupt, inefficient, dishonest, and in association with criminals.

The industries that had boomed so magnificently were strangely quiet. In particular, the two props of the economy, construction and automobiles, were down and out. The production of passenger cars fell by 75 percent in the three years from 1929 to 1932. The number of construction contracts fell by 60 percent between 1928 and 1932, but the value of the projects dropped by over 80 percent. Between 1928 and 1933, the amount of floor space in new buildings fell by 85 percent.

These statistics demonstrate the dimensions of the Depression. It was a nightmare world, an insane era when fear of taking a grip on things made matters worse.

In the United States and abroad, political leadership was inept. Politicians were swept along with events. Fortunately for the United States, the political structure was, and is, soundly based. No chance ever existed that the Constitution would be overturned, or debauched, as in Germany. The U.S. political processes, in fact, carried on as before. Suffering there was, a huge amount of it, that lasted year after year, but it was pain among millions of fellow sufferers.

The argument that those out of work were lazy devils, who just did not look for a job, was simply not valid in a time when fathers, uncles, brothers, sisters, aunts, and friends were in the same or a similar predicament.

Gradually, there came a realization that high unemployment was a national disgrace, that the government should not sit idly by trying to mend matters without changing fundamentally the structure of society.

President Herbert Hoover had his heart in the right place, as proved by his efforts to ease human suffering during and after World War I. Yet he failed in the task of mobilizing the country in her hour of need. The shocking years following the bull market crash of 1929 brought varied efforts from President Hoover, but none of them succeeded. He acted first as a cheerleader for business, then decided to let well enough alone and trust mainly to the ability of big business and finance to recover by themselves.

Today, this description of his efforts sounds callous and most unfair. It has to be remembered, however, that Hoover had operated all his life under a system that had succeeded better than any other in providing many of the good things of life for a majority of the people. Why change it? Why not continue to operate under the old methods that had proved so reliable in the past?

This argument was difficult to fault in the first few months of the stock market crash, even in the first year. Later, as unemployment grew, not only in the United States but in other lands as well, Hoover realized that something had to be done.

But he turned, in June 1931, to the troubles abroad, believing, as so many have done both before and since, that blaming foreign devils was easier than changing society at home.

Some justice attaches to Hoover's view. Then, as now, Europe could not be absolved from all responsibility in the financial and industrial crisis. The social structure of European countries was much less democratic than that of the United States. Statesmen and leaders in all walks of life in Europe came practically solidly from certain privileged families whose abilities were not always apparent at first glance, and whose haughty demeanor and patronizing airs and accents impressed only those who would fail to distinguish between chalk and cheese.

Indeed, the vindictiveness of the victorious Allies against Germany after World War I had come home to roost with a vengeance. Germany had been humiliated in the Treaty of Versailles that ended the war, but it did the Allies very little if any good, partly because the feeling of humiliation generated a desire among the German people for revenge and partly because the payment of vast reparations upset the financial stability of the nations involved. President Hoover proposed an international moratorium on war debts and reparations—the two curses that had threatened to put many countries in bankruptcy and had contributed signally to political instability in Europe. This bold move had its moment of success, but it came too late to prevent the financial collapse of Germany, while Britain went off the gold exchange standard.

The effect of these European events on the United States was profound. The U.S. banking system was in hands almost as aristocratic and closed as those that had succeeded so well in providing financial chaos in Europe. Many American banks, in fact, had family and business connections in

Europe, had invested heavily in foreign securities (notably bonds that were deemed secure), and now saw their investments almost vanish before their eyes.

What with the collapse in Wall Street, the inability of many businesses to pay off their bank loans, the bankruptcies of many of their customers, and the bank capital that was tied up in home mortgages that were in default, the American banking system was in a pretty bad way and rotten with personal corruption.

Here again, something had to be done. Once again, Hoover went through the usual channels for suggestions, this time to the very bankers that controlled the banking world, or much of it.

The hope that the strong banks would help the weak banks did not apply in practice, because the strong banks were in desperate need of help themselves and plainly saw the writing on the wall—the writing that spelled collapse.

Nor did President Hoover's Reconstruction Finance Corporation (RFC) provide the winning touch. This corporation was to pump federal money into the banking system and industry, thereby stimulating output and employment. It was the so-called trickle-down theory at work; in short, help industry on its feet again, and industry will then pass on the benefits to those looking for work.

But economic recovery takes time. The RFC, proposed in 1931, helped stem the flood of bank failures. But the effort came too late. In 1931, over two thousand banks, with deposits of over $1.5 billion dollars, suspended payments.

Thousands more banks followed suit in 1932 and 1933. The banking system had reached the point of collapse. A bank fails when it does not have enough money to honor the claims of its depositors. It fails when it shuts its doors

"A Wise Economist Asks A Question." Bank failures often took personal savings when the victim also was unemployed in the depression. This cartoon by John McCutcheon won the 1932 Pulitzer prize. Copyright 1932, *Chicago Tribune*. Used with permission, world rights reserved.

to the public, in effect telling its depositors that they are now unable to withdraw their bank balances. The effect of these bank closings on business customers and the public generally was tremendous.

The financial structure of many banks had become unwieldy through holding companies. Banks' connections with nonbanking businesses had brought them great losses in the stock market and industry. Their assets had been tied up in too many inferior investments that proved either unmarketable when the money was needed or cashable only at a great loss.

President Hoover had tried and failed. President Franklin D. Roosevelt took over on March 4, 1933, the day a corrupt and inefficient banking system could no longer open its doors.

10. Presidential Contrast: Hoover and Roosevelt

No ASPECT OF human life is more interesting or puzzling than the way people react to new circumstances. Surprises are so common, in fact, that unpredictable is the best word to apply to even the most careful forecasts.

Consider the contrast between President Hoover, a Republican, and President Roosevelt, a Democrat. To begin with, they had quite dissimilar backgrounds.

Herbert Clark Hoover was born in West Branch, Iowa in 1874. His Quaker parents died during his childhood, and Hoover went to live with an uncle in Oregon.

He studied mining engineering while working his way through Stanford University, graduating, after four years, in 1895. Hoover went into mining, but at a very modest level—pushing a cart. His pay was $2 a day.

The future President must have had ability and determination, since he attracted attention in the engineering world. He formed his own firm in 1908, and he soon became a millionaire. In 1914, when he was worth $4 million—

a very considerable sum in those days—he was in London and was asked by the U.S. ambassador there to help organize the evacuation of the more than 100,000 Americans caught in Europe by the sudden outbreak of World War I.

Hoover later directed the relief of Belgium, which had been destroyed by the German advance, and carried on similar work after the war ended in 1918.

Hoover was back in the U.S. in 1919, and in 1921 he was appointed by President Harding to be secretary of commerce, a position he continued to hold under President Coolidge. During Hoover's years as head of the Department of Commerce, he showed his true political leanings in that he usually favored voluntary action by big business and big finance, as in the reform of alleged abuses, preferring to ask for cooperation, since he detested government compulsion and controls.

When President Coolidge chose to retire from politics in 1928, he gave his support to Secretary of Commerce Hoover, who was easily successful in his bid for the Presidency.

But the industrial boom that had helped push stock prices higher and higher was already faltering when President Hoover entered the White House, and within a few months an avalanche of disaster hit the nation. Hoover proved almost completely incapable of handling the situation. His ability, determination, compassion, and experience all failed him, because they came up against his deeply felt aversion to government regulation.

Consider, on the other hand, Franklin Delano Roosevelt, born in 1882 in Hyde Park, New York. His background was wealthy, and socially almost impeccable. Whereas Hoover's early education was uneven, Roosevelt's was standard for scions of prominent families—Groton and Harvard, followed by studies at the Columbia University School of Law. He was admitted to the bar, and became a member of an established New York law firm. Roosevelt did not have to work his way through college and begin work at $2 a day pushing a cart!

Roosevelt's political career began in 1910, when he became a successful candidate for the New York state senate, but his work there ended when President Wilson appointed him assistant secretary of the Navy in 1913— a post he held until 1920 when he became a Vice Presidential candidate and lost.

Roosevelt did not then return to New York state politics but went into private business. In 1921, he was stricken with polio and struggled for the rest of his life against this severe handicap.

By 1928, Roosevelt was ready to reenter active politics, competing successfully for election as governor of New York.

Roosevelt occupied that position when Wall Street crashed in 1929. He was reelected in 1930, and showed his true spirit by tackling with enormous gusto the problems that faced New York State as prosperity quickly gave way to unemployment and economic and financial disaster.

His Presidential chances were obvious—and he accepted them and won. In 1932 President Hoover was defeated, and both houses of the Congress became Democratic.

President Roosevelt's experience in New York State was transferred from the governor's mansion in Albany to the White House in Washington, D.C. Even so, he was regarded by some as an elegant playboy. The adjective may be considered correct but not the noun. Roosevelt had little

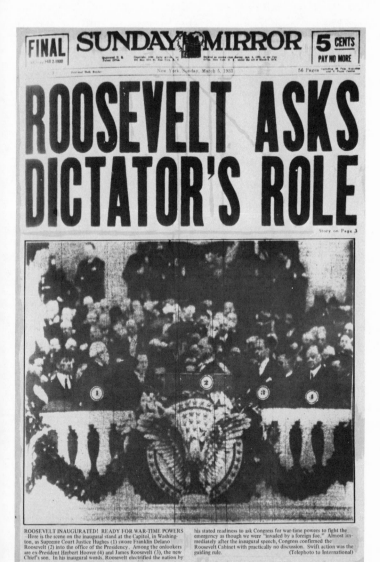

SUNDAY MIRROR

5 CENTS
PAY NO MORE

New York, Sunday, March 5, 1933.

56 Pages

ROOSEVELT ASKS DICTATOR'S ROLE

Story on Page 3

ROOSEVELT INAUGURATED! READY FOR WAR-TIME POWERS —Here is the scene on the inaugural stand at the Capitol, in Washington, as Supreme Court Justice Hughes (1) swore Franklin Delano Roosevelt (2) into the office of the Presidency. Among the onlookers are ex-President Herbert Hoover (4) and James Roosevelt (3), the new Chief's son. In his inaugural words, Roosevelt electrified the nation by his stated readiness to ask Congress for war-time powers to fight the emergency as though we were "invaded by a foreign foe." Almost immediately after the inaugural speech, Congress confirmed the Roosevelt Cabinet with practically no discussion. Swift action was the guiding rule. (Telephoto to International)

The *Sunday Mirror* front page, March 5, 1933.

of the playboy in him when it came to running the nation. He was wily, tough, and ruthless. He did not hesitate to use the existing powers of the Presidency and to extend them—although one of his major schemes, the 1933 National Industrial Recovery Act that spawned the National Recovery Administration (NRA), was later to be declared unconstitutional and was never replaced.

Contrast this with the efficiency of President Hoover, who believed in voluntarism, which conspicuously failed.

To what extent did the opposing social backgrounds of the two Presidents bear on the way they tackled the problems that emerged from the chaos of the stock market crash?

Did Roosevelt have a sense of guilt about his so-called aristocratic background in a professed democracy? Did he really have great compassion for the "forgotten man," * or did this compassion merely reflect his uneasiness about his social privileges? Did Roosevelt feel that he would not have succeeded had he come from a poorer home? Did that give him sympathy for those who struggled against unemployment and distress?

On the other hand, did President Hoover's self-made career make him feel that others could do the same if only they would get up and try? Or did he really believe that government rules and regulations would destroy the very economy that had given him such a successful career in more than one field? Is that why he believed with such passion in voluntarism? Or was there some sort of psychological block that prevented Hoover from admitting that the economic situation was so bad that private action and

---

* Roosevelt used this phrase, in his radio address of April 7, 1932, referring to the man at the bottom of the economic pyramid.

voluntarism would never work properly again? Was there, on Hoover's part, an unwillingness to help others, which stemmed from a serious fault in his psychological makeup?

Obviously, President Hoover was a conservative while President Roosevelt was a liberal. Conservatism is often puzzling to those with liberal tendencies, while liberalism is often frightening to those with conservative views.

Somehow, President Hoover was almost incapable of using the government to help others, especially those in distress. Even when faced with the greatest economic calamity in the nation's history, he much preferred helping the public via big business on the old trickle-down theory instead of making a fresh attack on the problems.

President Roosevelt would have little of that. He had showed what he thought of the trickle-down theory when, as governor of New York State, he established the nation's first state relief agency. Roosevelt believed in helping those who needed it—not only or mainly in helping business and finance to revive in the hope that those unemployed would sooner or later obtain jobs.

One wonders how anyone can tolerate human suffering when immediate relief is possible. What possible excuse is there? A belief in a certain political stance is hardly justification for continuing an injustice or evil that can be remedied. As a rule, of course, those who do not need help tend to object to letting the state help others. Yet when their own circumstances change and they themselves need aid, their own welfare is uppermost in their mind.

Actually, the contrast between Presidents Hoover and Roosevelt is not too unusual. A similar one, in fact, was obvious between President John F. Kennedy, who came from a well-to-do family, and President Richard M. Nixon, who struggled up from fairly poor circumstances. Here again, the comparatively wealthy President was more liberal than the self-made President.

Perhaps the *type* of education has something to do with it, since well-to-do children tend to be educated in liberal arts subjects while poorer children have to get down to the nuts and bolts of being trained to earn a living.

Rich liberals, when distributing government money, are accused of using funds in the way they spent their father's patrimony—without too much thought for the future. But what boggles the imagination in the case of Presidents Hoover and Roosevelt is Hoover's unwillingness to budge from his main political concepts even when disaster stared the nation in the face. One can understand a loyalty to established and successful beliefs, but, in the face of calamity, how can this be distinguished from callousness and stupidity?

The effects of the Wall Street crash were obvious on all sides. Stock and bond prices had collapsed. Businesses were bankrupt. Banks were staggering from defaulted loans and bad investments. Unemployment was high and rising. Personal and social distress were in clear evidence. Farmers were leaving the stricken land by the thousands. One did not need a magnifying glass to study the problem, since it was not only national but worldwide.

When commerce, business and finance are coming apart at the seams, the President's duty is to face reality, not shelter behind views that no longer hold good under changed circumstances.

The idea that any nation will go bankrupt, or become corrupt, or turn into a third-rate power, or degenerate into evil simply by helping those that are hungry, unemployed, sick, poor, badly housed, and clad in rags—this is an idea too foolish to need correction.

A nation that expects her people to fight in wars, and if necessary to give their lives for national survival, is morally bound to help those same people when they are in distress. This simple moral obligation that a state has to the people was lost on President Hoover but not on President Roosevelt.

In essence, the difference between the two Presidents was one of belief. Hoover believed that the state's duty was to provide a nation in which people are free to pursue their own ends without government interference. Roosevelt believed that the people are the state. History has proved how right Roosevelt was.

11. The Road to Recovery: The New Deal

THE ROAD TO RECOVERY was long and hard. In fact, it may be said to have lasted until the United States entered World War II in 1941. Until then, unemployment was high and not too many Americans were enjoying what was later to be known as full employment and prosperity.

The recovery itself may be divided into three parts for ease of examination:

—Socially, plans were needed to counter both the impact of unemployment in industry and the distress that farmers went through as low prices for their crops, and the dust storms, created misery.

—Economically, industry and finance had to be got moving again. This was no easy task even though President Roosevelt was an admirer of the British economist, J. M. Keynes, who believed in government action when private enterprise was falling down on the job.

—Protection is the third aspect, in that it was obviously vitally necessary to create new conditions of confidence under which industry, finance, and farms would operate. This included, of course, protection for investors in stocks and bonds, protection for bank depositors, protection for farmers against low prices and the dust bowls, and some protection for industry that was clearly at the mercy of many economic winds at home and from abroad. So, in some respects, protection meant reform.

Let us take a brief look at the general picture of the slump from 1929 to 1933. During this period, when the population was rising steadily from nearly 122 million to well over 125 million, the national income paid out to all recipients, such as salary and wage earners, fell by over 40 percent. Salaries alone dropped by over 45 percent, and wages by about 60 percent. Dividends were over 60 percent lower.

In the stock markets, disaster existed. Prices reached almost vanishing point. Consolidated Cigar common stock fell from over 100 to 3½. General Foods did better, dropping only from nearly 82 to less than 20. General Motors, that hero of the automobile boom, slid rapidly from over 91 to less than 8. U.S. Steel, the bulwark of heavy industry, obliged its stockholders by declining from over 261 to just over 21. Radio Corporation of America, which had sailed onward into the radio age on golden winds, fell to 2½ from nearly 115, causing a lot of financial static in the process. Wright Aeronautical flew like a lead balloon from nearly 150 to less than 4.

The railroad stocks did their best to emulate the industrial stock disaster. New York Central Railroad stock did its best to hit the bull's-eye of defeat by skidding from over 256 to less than 9. Southern Railway common fell from 165 to 2½, a decline of over 98 percent. Erie Railroad common stock slid from 93½ to exactly 2, an achievement that was surpassed by the many stocks that disappeared entirely, never to return, thereby obtaining a 100-percent decline.

The stocks mentioned above were not the inferior securities known in Wall Street as "cats and dogs." Most of these, of course, went squawking into the night, leaving behind no more than the screech of painful memories and missed opportunities in Wall Street, the street of regrets.

What is much clearer now than in the Depression, or for a few years thereafter, is the similarity of the 1929 crash and Depression to those that went before. True enough, these were so much bigger as to be in a separate category, but basically they were the same old crash and decline writ large.

Above all, the mentality of the business world had not kept pace with the growth in industry and finance. Too many financiers and businessmen still regarded themselves as legally entitled to plunder the public via banks (where the public kept its savings), the stock market (where the public bought and sold investments), and the commodity exchanges (where farmers and others bought and sold produce such as wheat and cotton.)

Farm prices in the United States did not fall so heavily as prices on the stock market, but what happened was disastrous to farmers. Wheat, for instance, fell by more than 60 percent.

So the Depression hit hard at most segments of business life. In fact, the market economy collapsed. It was not just the boom in the stock market that had turned into a panicky chaos. The whole world of capitalism—which had grown rapidly for one hundred years, suffering every now and again the spasms of recession, depression, and financial panic—had gone on its final spree, combining in the stock market boom, collapse, and the subsequent depression the finest mania of its kind in history.

Vigorous action was obviously the order of the day, and that is what occurred, basically through President Roosevelt and his program for economic recovery, which came to be known as the New Deal.

Roosevelt approached the nation's problems directly, right from the start of his administration. In his inaugural address on Saturday, March 4, 1933, the President put the blame where he thought it lay—on those who controlled business and on "the money changers who have fled." * His call to action to get the people back at work, and with a sound currency, elicited the strong support of Congress and the people.

Fast action followed. Within a few days, banks started opening again. Quickly, laws were passed, and steps taken administratively, to initiate a new program of economic and financial reform within the framework of new governmental responsibility for the welfare of the people.

Today, all this is taken for granted by most Americans. Even then, the New Deal was widely accepted by a nation grateful for decisive leadership and, above all, for the effective action that swept away old concepts of laissez faire under which industry, finance, and the people were supposed to always be able to take care of everything without very much government help.

In brief, the federal government forsook its old ways of nonintervention in the financial, social, industrial, and agricultural aspects of American life. It now accepted very

* Roosevelt's inaugural address is given in the Appendix.

real responsibility for the national welfare, even for the development of sections of the country under programs too big for private enterprise to tackle.

Confidence, of course, is the main prop of a society based on private finance and private business; without confidence, investors will not invest, bankers will not lend, and business will not expand. The confidence restored by President Roosevelt's inaugural address, together with the subsequent action taken by his administration and Congress, soon produced results.

The change in the nation was remarkable. Recovery was felt to be on the way. Bankers wanted to reopen as soon as possible to start earning money again. Washington attracted many trained people eager to participate in reshaping America. Some of the best of them were pressed into service by the President as his so-called Brain Trust. Today, this Brain Trust would probably be known as a "think tank" to assist national development. Meanwhile, Congressional legislation was prepared to deal with the many and often complex plans and programs then under discussion.

A major step in the road to economic recovery was taken when President Roosevelt, soon after taking office, decreed a temporary ban on the export or hoarding of gold, leading to the gradual devaluation of the dollar during the rest of 1933 and into 1934. This meant that the dollar was worth less in terms of gold. The value of the dollar internationally, of course, means a great deal to the import and export trade. If the dollar is valued at too high a rate, American goods cost too much and other nations won't buy them. An overvalued dollar also makes imports cheaper than they should be, so imports are bought and have to be paid for with dollars that otherwise would be spent on domestic goods.

Dollar devaluation stimulated foreign demand for American goods and helped bring about the domestic inflation that the President believed was needed to bring about industrial recovery. Inflation, or rising prices, is often regarded as very bad for a nation, but that is when inflation becomes excessive and lasts for a long time. A little bit of inflation, coming at the right time in a economic depression, can help a great deal in getting industry on the move again.

So prices started rising and businessmen felt a lot more confident. The prices of stocks on the stock exchanges rose, and investors began to feel a little happier. Businessmen gave orders for goods before the prices went even higher. So the wheels of industry started turning rather faster than before, but the process was gradual in the months and years after President Roosevelt took office.

Economically, then, industry was moving up again—not very fast, to be sure, but at any rate it was moving in the right direction after years of slump. That by itself was enough to convince many if not most Americans that President Roosevelt was the right man in the right job at the right time.

At the same time, farmers had to be helped on the road to recovery. Commodity prices were low, and many farmers had been forced to leave their farms not only by poor farm prices and consequent bankruptcy but by the dust bowls and storms that added to their anguish.

The New Deal aided farmers with legislation aimed at raising the prices of their farm products. Prices, of course, are a result of supply and demand. Too much output reduces prices. Cutting the output helps to raise prices. Farmers were offered money to leave some part of their farms unplanted. In this way, the farmers received federal money for *not* planting crops, and, since supplies were smaller, they also obtained higher prices for the crops they harvested.

So before long, the banks had been reopened, prices in general were rising, business was improving, and farmers were more confident of the future than they had been in years. Recovery, at least to some extent, had clearly arrived.

The improvement in industry helped to relieve unemployment, but something had to be done to directly assist those millions, including many younger people, who still needed jobs. President Roosevelt fashioned many schemes with this end in mind. Thousands were employed by the Civilian Conservation Corps (CCC), which helped restore areas ravaged by erosion. The President had a great interest in the conservation movement and in the rehabilitation of the nation's natural resources.

A public works program for the building of bridges and dams was also put into effect by the Roosevelt administration. However, it takes time to draw up plans for items such as these, and it takes even longer for this sort of money to trickle down into the pockets of the unemployed, partly because many of those people are simply not skilled in the building of bridges and dams, or they may not live in the regions that need such structures.

So some of this money went instead into relief payments to the unemployed, many of whom had been out of work for years and had also lost money in the stock market and in banks.

Another aim of the New Deal was to help property owners with mortgages. This was especially urgent since many mortgages on homes and farms had been taken out when business was prosperous, interest rates were comparatively high, and the borrowers confident that they would be able to meet the interest due plus capital repayments. When the stock market collapse was accompanied by the Depression, many of those with mortgages were forced to give them up and were sold out, thus losing their homes or farms.

In the dust storms of 1930s, farms in Oklahoma, Kansas, and other western states had to be abandoned. *Photo courtesy U.S. Dept. of Agriculture.*

The federal government came to the aid of these unfortunate people. The mortgages were refinanced through federal agencies, the interest rate was lowered, and a federal guarantee was given to safeguard those who had originally issued mortgages to the borrowers.

But has the importance of the New Deal been overrated?

The term itself was used for the first time by Roosevelt at the Democratic Convention in Chicago on July 2, 1932 when he promised: "I pledge myself . . . to a new deal for the American people." Raymond Moley, a professor at Columbia University in New York City and later to be head of the new President's Brain Trust, was an adviser to then Governor Roosevelt. It was he who coined the expression, New Deal, which came to be applied to the whole program of relief, recovery, and reform.

Some historians prefer to say that there were two New Deals. The first, according to this view, lasted from Roosevelt's 1932 speech in Chicago to 1935, when a radical shift in policies was made. So the second New Deal may be said to have lasted until Roosevelt died in 1945, even though, after 1941, the President was more concerned with America's role in World War II than with social and economic reform.

The first New Deal that in practice lasted only two years, from 1933 to 1935, helped alleviate the cruelties of the Depression, but big business and the U.S. Supreme Court did not always see eye to eye with the President, and Roosevelt became convinced that something else was needed. The second New Deal turned from industrial recovery and agrarian reform to measures designed to help labor and urban groups generally.

We see this gradual development of the New Deal by looking at the legislation. The early laws dealt with agriculture, national industrial recovery, the Tennessee Valley Authority, the issuance and sale of securities, and reform of banking. These were accompanied by financial and monetary policies designed to raise domestic prices and stimulate business and the economy.

Looking back now, we see how the early New Deal changed the face of the nation—literally, in fact, as in the case of the many extensive projects undertaken by the Tennessee Valley Authority.

But the *total* effect of all the New Deal was much more than recovery from the stock market collapse and the Depression. The nation was given a new way of life, a new way of looking at social and economic problems.

The impact of the federal government on national life was enormously increased, partly by later legislation but also by the new and heavier taxes that were used by the government to finance a vast range of federal subsidies for agriculture, small business, urban housing, and shipping, as well as to provide jobs for the unemployed. In addition, the government acquired new powers over private businesses, and developed social (security) insurance and old-age and unemployment assistance.

The federal government began to spend more money than it took in from taxes and had to borrow the balance, a process known as deficit financing. The bugaboo of balanced versus deficit budgets still plagues the nation, but not so persistently as before. Pump-priming of the economy, a name given to government efforts to generally stimulate business, became commonplace.

In brief, the New Deal ended the old belief in a limited federal government, and it subordinated private interests to the public welfare through the increased power and authority of the federal government. Much greater equality in wealth and income was achieved to the dismay and anguish of many of the wealthy. Economic planning on a national and regional scale came through federal authority.

We understand more clearly now that Hoover was un-
lucky in holding office as President at the time he did, in
that he had to ride out the economic storm. Roosevelt was
lucky in entering the White House when the worst was
just about over.

So the recovery that the normal business cycle had already put into being was aided by the New Deal, which
itself later became a much more comprehensive program of
economic and social reform than was required to deal with
the emergency of the Depression.

The New Deal and the recovery must be assessed against
the background of the business cycle—which notably came
to Roosevelt's aid—and with due consideration for the
ability of much of industry and finance to make a partial
recovery on their own, aided by Roosevelt's robust confidence and strong financial measures and reforms. This
does not detract from Roosevelt's achievements. It does
emphasize, however, that great national leaders are not
miracle men, but are people capable of bringing out the
best in their fellow countrymen.

Roosevelt held office longer than any other President.
(Constitutionally, such a period in office is no longer
possible.*) Much can happen to a nation in twelve years.
The mood of the people can change greatly. New dangers
can arise, both at home and abroad. Presidents, too, change.
President Roosevelt must have changed. But we shall never
know how he would have fared as President in a peaceful
and prosperous nation, because war intervened. A President
who had already achieved greatness by his ability to handle

* The 80th Congress proposed a Constitutional Amendment, Article
XXII, in 1947, providing that no person may serve as President for
more than two terms. The amendment was ratified by the requisite number
of states by 1951, in which year it officially became law.

a massive crisis at home was faced with a menace from abroad in the shape of the German Nazis and the Japanese, the latter attacking at Pearl Harbor. The nation was then at war. The New Deal began to fade in memory as the country harnessed its military might.

12. Effect of the Crash on the Future: Corrective Measures, Laws, and Controls

THE FINANCIAL ODOR out of Wall Street and banking circles filled the nation's air after the 1929 crash, and it grew more putrid as the years passed, the Depression arrived, and banking scandals were disclosed. The Augean stables of finance certainly needed a thorough cleansing. But, as so often happens in history, people are remembered as symbols of a morally bankrupt system, since their crimes were many and various, extending over many years, and far too complex to be fully described here.

Consider, for example, such corrupt titans of finance as Albert H. Wiggin of the Chase National Bank, Charles E. Mitchell of the National City Bank, and Richard Whitney, who for many years had been the president of the New York Stock Exchange. Jesse L. Livermore, gambler extraordinaire, had a book published shortly before he committed suicide; the book was entitled *How to Trade in*

Stocks. Dozens of others in business, banking, and the stock market found lasting relief in a leap from a bridge, in poison, or in gassing. (Not that the United States was the only one engulfed in startling revelations of sordid scandal and personal corruption. In Britain, for example, Clarence Hatry, the financier, had been put behind bars in 1930 for issuing stock that did not exist and for sundry other feats of the imagination. The Swedish match king, Ivar Kreuger, preferred a bullet below the heart when his Swedish Match Company was wrecked by speculation and fraud.)

A housecleaning was clearly overdue. Neither business nor finance can operate successfully under such corruption. The boom days, of course, had seen deceit successfully hidden under apparent achievements that often were widely applauded. The market crash, the Depression, and the banking collapse revealed only too clearly that many men of financial distinction were men of moral straw.

Financial reform was a must. The sheer magnitude of the stock market crash made strong legislation inevitable. Congress passed such legislation. The Securities Act of 1933 (popularly known as the Truth-in-Securities Act) for example required issuers of stocks and bonds to give much more information than formerly about the securities they were offering to the public. The Banking Act of 1933 made it unlawful for banks to have the notorious "security affiliates" through which stock gambling with bank funds had been possible. The Securities Exchange Act of 1934 regulated stock market trading. This act, along with the Securities Act of 1933, gave investors more information about what they were buying; gave them better protection when buying and selling on the stock exchanges; and out-

106 THE STOCK MARKET CRASH OF 1929

lawed such practices as bear raids, and insider transactions that worked against those on the outside, such as the small investor.

These legislative actions were followed by the Public Utility Holding Company Act of 1935, which compelled financial simplicity in a group that had become unbelievably complex in capital structure, as well as operationally.

The Trust Indenture Act of 1939 was passed because quite often the trustee, responsible for protecting the interests of investors, had failed to do so since his loyalties were split between the debtor and the investors. The law required the indenture (document) to specify the rights of the holders of securities such as bonds, and it imposed high standards of conduct on the trustee.

The Investment Company Act of 1940, and the Investment Advisers Act of 1940, regulated the practices of investment companies and the activities of investment advisers.

The securities business became subject to control by the Securities and Exchange Commission (SEC). This was a most important step, in that the regulation of Wall Street had been fought desperately by the aristocrats of finance who believed in the divine right of those with money. In brief, the Securities and Exchange Commission was a policeman provided to patrol the activities of Wall Street. It was to determine the adequacy of data supplied to the public, make rules to help the investor help himself, prevent sellers of securities from making fancy forecasts of future earnings, refuse to accept dubious statements, and, in short, insure minimum standards of behavior. In future, the investor would be allowed to make a fool of himself, but others would find it harder to make him look foolish.

Furthermore, the Federal Reserve Board received authority to fix margin requirements on the trading of securities, making it more difficult for speculation to rise uncontrollably, since investors could be forced to pay a larger deposit—even the full price—when buying securities.

The fact that so many laws had to be passed, and that so much else had to be done, publicly and privately, indicates not only the extent of the dishonesty and chaos but the outrage of an angry people.

The banking structure was cleansed but not healed. Its many weaknesses of structure could not be corrected immediately. However, the Banking Act of 1933 certainly helped assure that, in future, banks would no longer operate commercial banking along with investment banking. So some banks, such as Chase and National City, disposed of their security affiliates through which they had gambled heavily and lost. The House of Morgan itself was split in two and became a commercial banking house.

Even more important than what was done to correct immediate abuses was the change in attitude on the part of the American public as well as of those in financial and banking circles.

In 1929, few investors would have thought, or wished, that stock market transactions would soon be closely supervised by a government agency. The crash changed all that.

Too many had lost too much in the stock market débâcle, and too many depositors had seen their banks go out of business entirely, simply closing their doors for good, being legally dissolved and having nothing with which to repay their customers' savings.

Here we see, of course, the constant clash between freedom and regulation. The freedom had proved too heady, so regulation came in the wake of the disaster in stocks and in banks. Later, the early reforms were enhanced and consolidated by further measures that put both banks and securities firms under closer public watch. Likewise, the New York Stock Exchange, still the most important organized stock exchange and then the mainstay of the securities business, changed its own rules and regulations to provide a more professional and orderly market that helped the brokerage houses themselves, as well as investors, since more and more Americans became interested in stock market investing as greater opportunities for secure investments were made available through detailed information and honest trading.

Broader financial questions also must be considered. Because many banks had become bogged down with mortgages that could not be paid off, agencies of the federal government had to be set up to refinance farm and home mortgages. As a result of those actions, the federal government now has an enormous impact on the home-building industry—for instance, with its regulated interest rates, federal guarantees on insured mortgages, and the supply of billions of dollars.

Of greater international and national impact was the devaluation of the dollar. Britain was already off the gold exchange standard when President Roosevelt decided in April 1933 to suspend the convertibility of the dollar into gold and to allow the dollar to float. In January 1934, the fixed price of $35 an ounce for gold became law, in effect devaluing the dollar in terms of gold by about 41 percent.

This inflationary boost helped business and gave the stock market a much needed stimulus, considering the very depressed level of prices. Dollar devaluation and increased government spending were obviously helping the economy.

Today, we take it for granted that the government has control over national economic and financial policies, that bank deposits should be insured and thus secured, that stock operators should not be allowed to fleece the public with impunity, and that banks should not mix banking with gambling in the stock market. The current system, of course, is not perfect and never will be. Abuses still exist and no doubt always will, but the stock market crash of 1929 and the banking fiasco of 1933 made certain that never again would financial circles be operated for the benefit of those with wealth and at the expense of those without.

We see now, of course, that government regulation can never entirely replace the need for investors to consider carefully where they put their money. Even now, scandals arise in banks and brokerage houses, but they are small compared with those that were accepted as normal in the heady days up to 1929. In those days, an aristocracy of finance existed that viewed almost with contempt the small investor and small depositor, regarding them as fair game in amassing fortunes.

Today, the rich and the poor still exist, but the nation is mainly middle-class, and tens of millions of investors and bank depositors are happily unaware of what went on in the 1920s.

The major stock market decline of 1969–70 also brought into the open many abuses and caused the collapse of dozens of brokerage houses. That sharp setback brought into being a program for investors similar to the insurance of bank deposits—a clear indication that federal controls and regulations are essential in an industry where the opportunity for abuses is great, yet which, at the same time, is absolutely essential to the workings of the entire economic and financial system.

PART 2

FOR DISCUSSION

13. Was It Inevitable, and Can It Happen Again?

THE CRASH OF 1929 stands out in financial history like a lighted beacon on a hilltop warning of impending trouble. Was it inevitable? Can it happen again?

Stock market booms do not occur in business slumps. The greater the national prosperity, the greater the chance of a speculative boom. The bigger the boom, the bigger the slump.

The stock market boom leading up to 1929 was part of the national mood that had been generated by success in World War I, by the growing importance of the United States as world leader, and by the real prosperity that attended the 1920s.

The nation, of course, is far wealthier today than then. More people today have the good life. In fact, looking back on how people lived then, we are not too impressed. Perhaps others will be saying the same about us in the next century.

So the nation, by and large, was in good shape. The

113

economy was booming. A new era of freedom had come into being following the war. New inventions such as the automobile and radio were being mass-produced so that millions could buy them. Productivity per worker, or output per man-hour, rose strongly in the 1920s. Workers were not only producing more but reaping the benefits of their increased output. Today, productivity is higher still.

So, in theory at least, another stock market boom is possible, and so is another crash.

The 1929 stock market boom was not inevitable. It could have been controlled to some extent. It happened in part because the New York Stock Exchange refused to regulate itself and because the federal government then had few powers.

Since 1929, and even since 1945, we have seen stock market rallies and booms that were followed by major market setbacks. Yet the economy as a whole has been on a much more even keel. Obviously, the stock market moves up and down much more violently than does the economy. A case in point is the recession in business in 1970, and the severe stock market slump that went with it. Economic activity declined only modestly, but the average stock of good quality fell about 40 percent. This sharp market decline must have had some impact on the economy, but it was difficult to measure and no great business setback followed.

It is clear from this that controlling stock market activity is extremely difficult. Today, as in the 1920s, the stock market can generate a huge head of steam despite all the means available to control it. This can occur in individual securities that seem to hold great promise, in certain industries that are said to have enormous potential, and even in securities as a whole, because a tendency exists for all stocks to rise in a bullish market.

If the market booms of 1968 and 1972 can even now be followed by the slumps of 1970 and 1973, it is clear that in 1929 any strong control of speculation was almost out of the question. In the years leading up to 1929, perhaps, something could have been done to control the growing speculation and enthusiasm.

But just what success would have been achieved is impossible to judge. One basic trouble lies in the need to take action early. Yet how easy it is to try to control a stock market boom only to bring on an economic slump!

The stock market, in fact, is the basic mechanism whereby industry is financed. A rising stock market enables business to finance its capital needs much more easily than when stocks are depressed. The two factors, finance (through the stock market) and business, are so intertwined that separating them is almost impossible. That is why stock market booms are usually allowed to proceed, since trying to moderate them draws resentment and objections from businessmen and investors.

From our current vantage point, we can see how difficult it would have been politically to control the stock market boom that got under way in the 1920s. Even now, when the federal government has so many more controls to limit speculation, the stock market can put on quite a show if investors really get excited about prospects. Even now, stocks can fall heavily in a very short time.

So the stock market boom of 1929 can be understood. So can the market slump that followed during 1929 and 1930.

What is puzzling is the extent of the decline and the way the economy went into a tailspin.

Prosperity triggered the stock market boom, and speculative arrangements at that time turned the boom into near hysteria. The nation's mood of buoyant optimism was heightened for many investors by participation in the stock market orgy of 1928 and 1929. Even so, a sharp drop in stock prices does not of necessity bring on a massive depression that lasts for a decade.

What caused the Depression to be so severe? One factor, of course, was the shattering of so much wealth in the stock market collapse. And apart from a rally in late 1929 and early 1930, the stock market collapse itself went on and on. It seemed never to end. Prices almost literally disappeared. Stocks sold at small fractions of their high boom prices.

The nation's mood must clearly have radically changed by 1932. The excitement of the 1920s had given way to fear, as savings were lost in the crash and unemployment grew. Other factors, of course, contributed to this change. Financial, business, and political trouble in Europe worried Americans and had a direct impact on the American stock market through sales of U.S. securities held abroad.

There was then, in 1929, a most unusual conjuncture of events. A recurrence is hardly likely, but it is possible. Certainly, the stock market as currently organized will go on buying sprees every so often and will suffer a collapse as the boom spends itself. We can be sure of that.

Nor is the national mood capable of being changed easily by government exhortation. So a really great bull market in stocks could be seen again in times of business prosperity. So could a crash, since that follows normally. The bigger the boom, the bigger the drop. Even if all securities had to be paid for in full when purchased, a big bull market in stocks could come along when industry is in high gear, personal savings are ample, worker productivity is rising, and the nation is looking ahead with confidence.

But a depression similar to that of the 1930s is much more unlikely. To say that it cannot happen again is to tempt fate.

We see all the time how nations, like people, act selfishly, putting their own interests first no matter how others are troubled, injured, and inconvenienced. International cooperation is still far from perfect. Fear and greed are just as much a part of the international scene today as they are of national life, social matters, and personal affairs. Also, other nations directly and indirectly affect the United States. Today, the United States is by far the strongest in the world, especially in the economic and financial sphere. But the position is changing. The future may find that U.S. industrial supremacy, for example, is being threatened by developments abroad. Likewise, U.S. business may be influenced greatly by foreign competition. We have seen this already, for instance in the mass production of automobiles in Japan for the American market. Many other examples can be cited, including oil supplies.

Even so, the recurrence of the Great Depression is hardly likely. The government has too many powers to control the economy and to stimulate industry and finance by increasing the money supply, granting tax relief, expanding public works, and paying higher social benefits generally. Deficit spending pumps money into the economy. So many built-in safeguards now exist that sending the economy into a tailspin would be a difficult feat even if deliberately attempted.

Today, the economy is far more prosperous than in the

1920s. Many new industries exist, of which television manufacture is but one and nuclear power generation is another.

Society also is far more democratic than in the 1920s, when so much wealth was held by the rich, and when financiers and businessmen regarded themselves as lords of creation well above the common man. Today, tens of millions of investors put their money into the stock market for income, security, and hopes of capital gains. Over the years, despite ups and downs, they have done well. They have seen their capital grow far faster than inflation has eroded the value of the dollar.

Investors gain, of course, by the growth of population and rising economic productivity. Stockholders are the main beneficiaries since they are, in fact, the owners of a company, take a chance on success, and reap the rewards of business improvement.

Investors are safeguarded as never before, but it is easy for them to lose capital; so many schemes exist to defraud, the market itself is given to feverish tantrums, and the ups and downs of business life are seen all the time.

The Securities Act of 1933 and the Securities Exchange Act of 1934 brought a new era to stock market finance. Under the 1933 act, as we have seen, public offerings of new securities are to be adequately described so that investors have a reasonable idea what the company does. The 1934 act regulates securities exchanges to prevent unfair practices. Officers, directors, and owners of 10 percent or more of a stock have to report their stock transactions. Dishonest practices, such as faked sales, are banned.

It sounds impressive and it is, compared with what went on in earlier years. Yet much remains to be done, in that new devices for cheating the public are constantly coming along.

One such device is the manipulation of balance sheets and earnings statements to show a better position than actually exists. In some cases, for instance, depreciation, or the loss in value of assets as they age, may be written off at a low rate, thus enabling earnings to look better than they actually should be. Many more complex schemes are available to those that wish to present an unfair picture of a company's financial status to the public.

Today, the investor is protected as never before, but the stock market drops of 1970 and 1973 disclosed many abuses, saw the collapse of dozens of brokerage houses, and put the savings of many investors in jeopardy. A new scheme to insure investments had to be devised. So greater protection is now available to investors.

The future will not bring easy and successful investment. Life is too complex for that, and the stock market reflects the changing structure of society along with the hopes, fears, and delusions of those with wealth.

The accelerating tempo of society, the rapid technological changes, the rising prosperity of industrial nations, and the constant willingness of so many investors to take a chance on something that looks good—all these make possible another 1929, especially if the controlling authorities, such as the Federal Reserve Board, are lax in their job.

It is one thing to say there can be another 1929, since in that year the stock market collapse was contained within manageable limits; the real damage came later as stock prices continued to drop and the economy went into a tailspin of defeat and despair. Therefore, another 1929 is possible, but not likely, while another 1932 is almost un-thinkable.

The United States has come a long way since the tragedy of mass unemployment and millions of hopeless humans. There are new ways of controlling the economy and of stimulating business and finance. Many safeguards exist in the form of pensions, social security payments, and government help for those in need. These help prop a faltering economy and help prevent a true recession. Great success has been achieved in this field, even though the stock market itself follows a course distinguished from the past only in degree.

Yet taking too much for granted would be most unwise. It once was argued that the big investors, such as mutual funds and pension funds, would help support the stock market in any decline. In the collapses of 1970 and 1973, however, these large investors were conspicuous by their absence. In fact, some helped the decline by massive sell-ing, even by selling stocks they did not have, in the hope of buying them back later at a profit.

So it pays to be on guard. In one sense, anything can happen, because society constantly changes and new con-ditions arise. No one can tell at this moment just what will happen in industry and finance over the next ten years. Or, in the field of international matters, what relationship will exist between Japan and China or between the United States and China in ten years' time? No one knows.

It is better to be watchful, not dogmatic, in that the stock market reflects all the news that affects stocks—and that is just about everything. People are still very much the same as in 1929. They still like a fling in the market, even with-out troubling to find out their chances of success.

Certainly, we shall see booms and slumps in the future, but we can hope that they will be nothing like the disaster in the stock market and in industry that followed the stock market crash of 1929.

14. What If No Crash Had Occurred?

HAD THERE BEEN no Wall Street crash in 1929, what would the country be like today?

Had the crash ended in 1929 with no major downturn in the economy, President Hoover could well have been reelected. Things would have changed to some extent, as they always do. Perhaps Franklin D. Roosevelt would have been elected later as President, but his New Deal would hardly have been as forceful as it was; even in reality, the New Deal itself was watered down considerably as the fears of disaster were replaced by hopes of survival.

The traumatic events of 1929 and subsequent years would never have occurred. The nation would now be unable to look back on the crash and the Depression in order to draw therefrom not only valuable lessons but the knowledge that this country can survive the worst. The trend in the United States is toward a stronger democracy and more social justice. The New Deal helped this process along; in fact, the Roosevelt reforms themselves rose from the ashes of economic and financial chaos.

Without doubt, the crash in Wall Street helped, if it did not entirely account for, the downturn in economic activity that within three years had the nation almost helpless. It follows then that, without the crash, a New Deal would hardly have been possible. Even so, the New Deal accomplished in a hurry what probably would have occurred anyway over a longer period. In fact, it is possible that, in the two decades following the 1929 crash, as much would have been achieved slowly as was accomplished quickly by the social and economic explosion that opened up the great gaps in national life through which the New Deal came. Only a force as great as the crash and the Depression combined could possibly have shattered so easily the hold that men of wealth had on the nation in the 1920s. Their grip was something to behold, as was the arrogant use of their power.

A great inequality of income existed. Also, except for a few years in the 1920s and the years during and since World War II, there never really was any general national prosperity. The American people lived well compared with those in other countries, but many of them suffered poverty and other deprivations.

Such social injustice would have had to be tackled sooner or later. As it was, the market crash speeded up the process. Had something similar occurred to influence the field of race relations, for instance, it is possible that race problems today would be less abrasive than they are.

The banking collapse was hastened by the Wall Street crash, because so many banks had suffered heavily in their investments. That they held out until 1933 before final buckling under the strain is testimony to many factors, including the help they got from the government, the sta-

President Roosevelt signing the emergency Banking Act of March 9, 1933. *Courtesy Franklin D. Roosevelt Library.*

124

bility of many banks, and the way the American people conducted themselves in the face of economic and financial defeat.

Certainly, the banking structure was unsound for many years before the banks closed their doors, but it was not so shaky that the stock market slump forced an immediate collapse. Most banks and bankers held on grimly during both the stock market crash and the subsequent Depression. Here, too, changes would have come without any market collapse, and they would have come much more quietly and with far less social upheaval.

Industrial corporations were top-heavy in their financial structure. The device of the holding company enabled companies to pyramid their subsidiaries alarmingly. A small amount of trouble in one part of corporate life could trigger massive reactions elsewhere. Little trouble was seen as the stock market roared along the path to what proved to be disaster. When the stock market crashed, the pyramids became shaky, then toppled. Fortunately, many industries were not in the holding company game, but the holding companies were powerful factors among utilities and railroads. When the actual operating companies suffered business reverses, the holding companies could hardly pay their bond interest. The stock market crash simply wiped out the holding companies. Without a crash, the holding companies would have held out longer, but, over a longer period, reform would have come.

Today, we are accustomed to masses of statistics. The United States is just about the best situated from that viewpoint even though much remains to be done. But, back in the 1920s and the 1930s, comparatively few figures were available to judge the trends in the economy. Not that more statistics would necessarily have made a major difference, in that many industries then had their own data-collecting departments, and, in any event, collecting statistics and using them wisely are two different things.

The market crash certainly stimulated economic investigation. More details were needed of the working of a complex economic system. Without the crash, less energy would have gone into this comparatively new activity, which at best may be described as a cross between a science and an art.

The crash also brought a new understanding of the complexities of international finance in the national and corporate spheres. Huge debts among nations helped bring on the chaos, especially those debts associated with such an unproductive activity as World War I. American bankers and investment firms saw their foreign investments shrink in the Depression and as political upheavals hit many European countries. A new awareness of foreign problems developed. Caution replaced haste.

The crash, like all bad things, had a tendency to create improvements in many walks and aspects of life. Even so, the United States would probably be better off today had it not occurred.

The 1929 crash by itself was not very much compared with what followed. The total suffering of the subsequent years was immense. The nation's history is scarred by the memory. The crash of 1929 and the Depression are still strong in our collective consciousness. They will never go away entirely, since the American people's memories of them are always revived when the stock market slumps or when the economy enters what appears to be a severe recession. The nation would perhaps be better off without the memories of those painful years; nevertheless, the lessons learned, and the action taken to help prevent anything similar happening again, prove that men can gain from misfortune.

15. Suppose Franklin D. Roosevelt Had Become President in 1929

WHAT WOULD HAVE HAPPENED if Franklin D. Roosevelt had become President of the United States in 1929 instead of 1933?

There is no telling, but it is highly likely that the stock market boom would have ended—in that all booms do sooner or later—but that it would have done so without having achieved the same final burst of insane speculation.

As for the constant sagging in stock prices that went on and on from 1930 to 1932, and the economic depression that sank its teeth into humanity for many a year leaving marks that still remain, the worst that can be said is that, under President Roosevelt, things could have been better but could not have been worse.

At least, some more effective action would have been taken—of that we can be sure. Just how effective it would have been, though, is anyone's guess. But it does seem reasonable to assume that, under Roosevelt, the stock market's decline might have been lengthened and so moderated in intensity, the Depression might have been curbed.

On balance, however, it is likely that President Roosevelt would not have been able to gain reelection in 1932. The reason for this is that the combination of the stock market collapse and a rich economy that was turning sour was simply too much for the mood of the time and for the shaky financial structure of banking and business. The international complications arising from unwise foreign lending by Wall Street, and the rotten financial structure in Europe stemming from World War I, did nothing to help.

President Roosevelt could not have changed overnight the squalid mess that by 1929 formed the main support of the towering expectations of the American people. This stock market boom was no minor event but the final spree of a people that had gradually become obsessed with wealth and its quick acquisition.

The stock market mania leading up to 1929 will go down in history with the other infamous examples of public delusions and rages. Most, if not all of them, had some reasonable basis for exciting the public interest. The public usually is not so foolish as to get enthusiastic about absolutely nothing. Few gold rushes, for instance, ever repay all the prospectors, not even in South Africa. Nor do diamond diggings. But, usually, some gold is there, some diamonds are found. The difference is one of degree, but, in public manias, the difference in degree is so great as to become in practice a difference in fact. Thus the stock market boom of 1929 was based on many factors, but mainly on the rising prosperity of the American people.

President Roosevelt was part of his time just as was

President Hoover. Roosevelt could not have come into office in 1929 and turned the stock rush into something reasonable and directly related in enthusiasm to the actual growth of American industry. He may have been able to moderate the final leg of the bull market, but, apart from that, the mania would have spent itself in about the same way.

Hardly conceivable, however, is the view that Roosevelt would have stood by almost idly, exhorting business, hoping for the best, meeting with representatives from various walks of life, and taking effective action only rarely and specifically and then without too much impact on the general economy.

One reservation must be noted. Men change in office. Men respond to opportunities. Men sense when something is possible, and when it is not.

Winston Churchill took over as prime minister in Britain when the outlook for his country, in the early days of World War II, was black. So did President Roosevelt in the United States, albeit in peacetime. Had either man assumed command earlier, their reputation may not have survived so easily.

Roosevelt had ample opportunity to study the market crash and the Depression, and to make plans well ahead. The "brains" he later assembled were thus enabled to carry out his general ideas and give them specific shape. But Roosevelt would not have been so fortunate had he taken office in 1929. It is one thing to study a situation from afar, and deal with it when the worst is at hand; it is quite another to change a situation as it develops.

President Hoover had that job. Things got steadily worse while he was in office. Instead of operating under favorable circumstances, he had to constantly assess a changing situation and devise new policies against the backdrop of a bewildered nation. That is a tough job at best.

What would President Roosevelt have done in President Hoover's position?

The confidence Roosevelt created in 1933 was quite unnecessary in 1929. Any attempt then to change the course of the boom would have been resisted by big business and big finance. Indeed, only in the Depression itself was anything substantial achieved. That, of course, is when Roosevelt was President. Yet President Hoover also was in office when conditions were really bad, and very little happened.

One major distinction between these two Presidents was Hoover's insistence that big business and the banking system should be helped first on the trickle-down theory. Roosevelt almost surely would have done something more to help the masses of unemployed who desperately needed immediate direct help and not indirect help sometime later.

The quality of a statesman is partly determined by how he responds to the real needs of his people. It is almost unthinkable that President Roosevelt would not have sensed, had he been in office from 1929 to 1933, the disaster that was gradually enveloping the nation.

It was all around President Hoover. The stock market crash and the growing economic setback were not delusions, or local matters of no national import. They were real. By the end of 1930, the souplines and breadlines, unemployment, apple salesmen, poverty and despair were in plain view, along with the low prices of stocks and the sagging economy.

Roosevelt, as President, would hardly have accepted

these the way President Hoover did. He would have done something, even if the old concepts of society and economics had to be broken.

The old order had to change. Hoover's stay in the White House saw a new order coming into being, whether or not he liked it. The system as known by Hoover was falling to bits as he watched, almost in mesmerized silence at times—or so it seems from his lack of effective action.

What was needed, even in 1930, 1931 and 1932, was the sort of national challenge given later by Roosevelt in his New Deal.

It is unlikely that Roosevelt would have developed the same plans for the New Deal had he been in Hoover's position. The nation obviously was unwilling to accept any great measure of governmental control in 1929, or earlier, since conditions were too favorable for financial success.

Even as the market fell, rallies occurred, stimulating hope that the worst was over. This constant sagging eroded hope time and again. Finally, Franklin D. Roosevelt was on hand when the stock market was down and out and the banks were closed. The final sag had occurred, and in stepped Roosevelt to turn the nation around. The coincidence was almost unbelievable.

Four years earlier, Roosevelt, had he been in office, would have faced booming prosperity. He too would have seen the speculative bubble burst and the economy turn sour. But the chances are that both the stock market crash and the Depression would have been nothing like so severe as they were under President Hoover, whose inability to change and unwillingness to act made him the last representative of an order that had finally overstayed its public welcome.

16. The Future

ONE OF THE STRANGE aspects of life is that events change their shape and significance as the years pass and new ideas take root. So it was, for example, that, in the early 1940s, the thought that another 1929 was possible was usually dismissed as fantasy. For one thing, the stock market was still depressed and many issues were still very much lower than they had been in 1929. Indeed, years were to pass before the market as a whole got back to the 1929 level, and by then, of course, inflation had made the dollar worth less, so stock prices should have been correspondingly higher.

What we have learned since the 1930s is that the stock market is always ready to take off if conditions encourage a buying spree. The public is always willing to gamble, if there is a remote chance of winning. We have learned too that controlling these urges is not easy, and that limiting speculation while not destroying confidence in the economy is a tricky and delicate business.

When the American economy is expanding and people are prosperous, there is always a reasonable chance that the stock market, in some of its parts, will have a speculative boom that almost rivals that of 1929. So a watchful eye has to be kept on the stock market and on the credit facilities available to speculators.

We also know that the old safeguards do not always work, that economics is a changing art (or science), and that what passed muster in the old days may not do so now. Society has not stopped changing. Industry progresses. So do methods of financing business.

Other countries can hurt the United States, but the major force in international relations is the American economy. The United States is now like an elephant in the rowboat of international trade and finance. A slight shift in position and the other countries in the boat are severely inconvenienced. It is not easy to maintain the domestic economy on an even keel, let alone international trade and finance. Cooperation with other countries is essential to stability in world affairs. At home, moderation and reason are required. Free enterprise is always on the move. In brief, it is a tough job to manage an economy so well that industrial output keeps rising, that inflation is kept to reasonable levels, and that unemployment has no severe impact on social life.

From this viewpoint, then, an economic downturn is always likely to occur sooner or later. The stock market will always boom and slump, since it measures, in essence, what is left to the owners of business after the bondholders have had their share. The balance varies sharply, and stocks often move violently in recognition of this fact.

Needed most in government, especially in the White House, is a flexible attitude and a reasonable approach. If the old methods do not work, they must be ditched after a reasonable try. Nothing suggests that the same remedy will cure all ills now and forever. New cures will be needed, sometimes drastic ones.

The world often seems a picture of chaos and despair, but the trend is up since the industrial nations are getting richer, and greater democracy and a finer social justice come from rising wealth and better education.

The torment that the United States endured during the Depression proved the stability of the Constitution and the flexibility of the political processes.

Nothing like the Depression should ever occur again. If it does, the fault will come from unwillingness to take action, from a fixed belief in the validity of certain theories, and from a hope that what worked well in an earlier generation will also work well again.

The old saying that a stitch in time saves nine applies with force to controlling speculation and a booming economy. The nation as a whole can produce only so much wealth. No country, no system, has found the means to rapidly stimulate national wealth, over a period of years, without facing either serious social problems or a dramatic setback. Wealth does not normally increase rapidly, but through the slow processes that increase industrial and agricultural productivity as the years pass. So any stock market boom that rapidly outpaces the economy is bound to collapse sooner or later. Any economy that is stimulated to excess will surely have setbacks that seriously undermine the future.

A few countries from time to time seem to be exceptions to this rule. Germany, Japan, and Italy roared ahead in the years after World War II, but the exhaustion of defeat in war put them low on the ladder when they began to recover. So their achievements must be reduced to that degree, and the pace also proved too hot to last.

The American economy can only achieve modest increases in living standards from year to year. That should be the goal of any administration. Even that is not easy to ensure.

Inflation too is a problem, in that, stimulating the economy can easily overheat the financial structure.

The stock market reflects basically the condition of the economy, and, over a longer period, the trend of inflation. National economic growth, plus inflation, plus the rise in population, are almost never greater than 10 percent per year, as shown in stock prices over a period of years.

A stock market that roars ahead as it did in 1928 and 1929 is simply outpacing reality. That is why a crash was inevitable when once the point of no return had been passed, long before September 1929.

The same can happen again—but only if reality is replaced by delusion.

Appendix. Franklin D. Roosevelt's First Inaugural Address

The following is a transcript of Franklin D. Roosevelt's inaugural address, delivered in Washington, D.C. on March 4, 1933, the day he took office in his first term as President.

I am certain that my fellow Americans expect that on my induction into the Presidency I will address them with a candor and a decision which the present situation of our nation impels. This is preeminently the time to speak the truth, the whole truth, frankly and boldly. Nor need we shrink from honestly facing conditions in our country today. This great nation will endure as it has endured, will revive and will prosper. So, first of all, let me assert my firm belief that the only thing we have to fear is fear itself—nameless, unreasoning, unjustified terror which paralyzes needed efforts to convert retreat into advance. In every dark hour of our national life a leadership of frankness and vigor has met with that understanding and support of the people themselves which is essential to victory. I am convinced that you will again give that support to leadership in these critical days.

In such a spirit on my part and on yours we face our common difficulties. They concern, thank God, only material things. Values have shrunken to fantastic levels; taxes have risen; our ability to pay has fallen; government of all kinds is faced by serious curtailment of income; the means of exchange are frozen in the currents of trade; the withered leaves of industrial enterprise lie on every side; farmers find no markets for their produce; the savings of many years in thousands of families are gone.

More important, a host of unemployed citizens face the grim problem of existence, and an equally great number toil with little return. Only a foolish optimist can deny the dark realities of the moment.

Yet our distress comes from no failure of substance. We are stricken by no plague of locusts. Compared with the perils which our forefathers conquered because they believed and were not afraid, we have still much to be thankful for. Nature still offers her bounty and human efforts have multiplied it. Plenty is at our doorstep, but a generous use of it languishes in the very sight of the supply. Primarily this is because rulers of the exchange of mankind's goods have failed, through their own stubbornness and their own incompetence, have admitted their failure, and abdicated. Practices of the unscrupulous money changers stand indicted in the court of public opinion, rejected by the hearts and minds of men.

True they have tried, but their efforts have been cast in the pattern of an outworn tradition. Faced by failure of credit they have proposed only the lending of more money. Stripped of the lure of profit by which to induce our people to follow their false leadership, they have resorted to exhortations, pleading tearfully for restored confidence. They know only the rules of a generation of self-seekers. They have no vision, and when there is no vision the people perish.

The money changers have fled from their high seats in the temple of our civilization. We may now restore that temple to the ancient truths. The measure of the restoration lies in the extent to which we apply social values more noble than mere monetary profits.

Happiness lies not in the mere possession of money; it lies in the joy of achievement, in the thrill of creative effort. The joy and moral stimulation of work no longer must be forgotten in the mad chase of evanescent profits. These dark days will be worth all they cost us if they teach us that our true destiny is not to be ministered unto but to minister to ourselves and to our fellow men.

Recognition of the falsity of material wealth as the standard of success goes hand in hand with the abandonment of the false belief that public office and high political position are to be valued only by the standards of pride of place and personal profit; and there must be an end to a conduct in banking and in business which too often has given to a sacred trust the likeness of callous and selfish wrongdoing. Small wonder that confidence languishes, for it thrives only on honesty, on honor, on the sacredness of obligations, on faithful protection, on unselfish performance; without them it cannot live.

Restoration calls, however, not for changes in ethics alone. This nation asks for action, and action now.

Our greatest primary task is to put people to work. This is no unsolvable problem if we face it wisely and courageously. It can be accomplished in part by direct recruiting by the government itself, treating the task as we would treat the emergency of a war, but at the same time, through this employment, accomplishing greatly needed projects to stimulate and reorganize the use of our natural resources.

Hand in hand with this we must frankly recognize the overbalance of population in our industrial centers and, by engaging on a national scale in a redistribution, endeavor to provide a better use of the land for those best fitted for the land. The task can be helped by definite efforts to raise the values of agricultural products and with this the power to purchase the output of our cities. It can be helped by preventing realistically the tragedy of the growing loss through foreclosure of our small homes and our farms. It can be helped by insistence that the federal, state, and local governments act forthwith on the demand that their cost be drastically reduced. It can be helped by the unifying of relief activities which today are often scattered, uneconomical, and unequal. It can be helped by national planning for and supervision of all forms of transportation and of communications and other utilities which have a definitely public character. There are many ways in which it can be helped, but it can never be helped merely by talking about it. We must act and act quickly.

Finally, in our progress toward a resumption of work we require two safeguards against a return of the evils of the old order; there must be a strict supervision of all banking and credits and investments; there must be an end to speculation with other people's money, and there must be provision for an adequate but sound currency.

These are the lines of attack. I shall presently urge upon a new Congress, in special session, detailed measures for their fulfillment, and I shall seek the immediate assistance of the several states.

Through this program of action we address ourselves to putting our own national house in order and making income balance outgo. Our international trade relations, though vastly important, are in point of time and necessity secondary to the establishment of a sound national economy. I favor as a practical policy the putting of first things first. I shall spare no effort to restore world trade by international economic readjustment, but the emergency at home cannot wait on that accomplishment.

The basic thought that guides these specific means of national recovery is not narrowly nationalistic. It is the insistence, as a first consideration, upon the interdependence of the various elements in and parts of the United States—a recognition of the old and permanently important manifestation of the American spirit of the pioneer. It is the way to recovery. It is the immediate way. It is the strongest assurance that the recovery will endure.

In the field of world policy I would dedicate this nation to the policy of the good neighbor—the neighbor who resolutely respects himself and, because he does so, respects the rights of others—the neighbor who respects his obligations and respects the sanctity of his agreements in and with a world of neighbors.

If I read the temper of our people correctly, we now realize as we have never realized before our interdependence on each other; that we cannot merely take but we must give as well; that if we are to go forward, we must move as a trained and loyal army willing to sacrifice for the good of a common discipline, because without such discipline no progress is made, no leadership becomes effective. We are, I know, ready and willing to submit our lives and property to such discipline, because it makes possible a leadership which aims at a larger good. This I propose to offer, pledging that the larger purposes will bind upon us all as a sacred obligation with a unity of duty hitherto evoked only in time of armed strife.

With this pledge taken, I assume unhesitatingly the leadership of this great army of our people dedicated to a disciplined attack upon our common problems.

Action in this image and to this end is feasible under the form of government which we have inherited from our ancestors. Our Constitution is so simple and practical that it is possible always to meet extraordinary needs by changes in emphasis and arrangement without loss of essential form. That is why our constitutional system has proved itself the most superbly enduring political mechanism the modern world has produced. It has met every stress of vast expansion of territory, of foreign wars, of bitter internal strife, of world relations.

It is to be hoped that the normal balance of executive and legislative authority may be wholly adequate to meet the unprecedented task before us. But it may be that an unprecedented demand and need for undelayed action may call for temporary departure from that normal balance of public procedure.

I am prepared under my constitutional duty to recommend the measures that a stricken nation in the midst of a stricken world may require. These measures, or such other measures as the Congress may build out of its experience and wisdom, I shall seek, within my constitutional authority, to bring to speedy adoption.

But in the event that the Congress shall fail to take one of these two courses, and in the event that the national emergency is still critical, I shall not evade the clear course of duty that will then confront me. I shall ask the Congress for the one remaining instrument to meet the crisis—broad executive power to wage a war against the emergency, as great as the power that would be given to me if we were in fact invaded by a foreign foe.

For the trust reposed in me I will return the courage and the devotion that befit the time. I can do no less.

We face the arduous days that lie before us in the warm courage of national unity; with the clear consciousness of seeking old and precious moral values; with the clear satisfaction that comes from the stern performance of duty by old and young alike. We aim at the assurance of a rounded and permanent national life.

We do not distrust the future of essential democracy. The people of the United States have not failed. In their need they have registered a mandate that they want direct, vigorous action. They have asked for discipline and direction under leadership. They have made me the present instrument of their wishes. In the spirit of the gift I take it.

In this dedication of a nation we humbly ask the blessing of God. May He protect each and every one of us. May He guide me in the days to come.

Glossary

BEAR   Any person who expects stock prices to go down

BEAR MARKET   A time of falling stock prices

BEAR RAID   An organized attempt by bears to force stock prices down in the hope of buying them back cheaper, thus making a profit, as in selling short.

BLUE CHIPS   Highly regarded securities, the allusion being to blue poker chips of high value

BLUE SKY LAWS   Government regulations to help protect investors against those promoters who would try to sell even the blue sky

BOND   A loan from an investor to a corporation, which agrees to pay interest on the loan

BULL   Any person who expects stock prices to go up

BULL MARKET   A time of rising stock prices

CATS AND DOGS   Very inferior securities of low price

CORNER   An attempt to control a stock or a commodity by buying up all the available supplies, thus forcing the price up and making a profit on the purchases

CURB   The former Curb Exchange that once operated actually on the street, or curb, but now has its own building and is known as the American Stock Exchange

DEPRECIATION   The fall in value of assets; also the annual charge made in a company's account for this loss of value over a certain period

143

DOG   A stock that is without popular interest and never moves very much

FEDERAL RESERVE BOARD (FRB)   Independent agency largely responsible for controlling the nation's money supply, but with many other duties relating to supervising banking and transactions in the securities markets

GOLD EXCHANGE STANDARD   A variety of the gold standard under which gold is used in international trade but not in transactions at home

GOLD STANDARD   A system of national and international finance under which gold is variously used to settle transactions, often with paper currency backed by and convertible into gold

HOLDING COMPANY   A company that holds stock in and controls other companies for business or financial reasons

INDENTURE   A document that spells out in detail the rights of the holders of such securities as bonds

LAISSEZ FAIRE   Freedom for individual action without government intervention

MARGIN   The deposit to be put down by stock traders

OVER-THE-COUNTER (OTC)   The stock market that operates via telephone, not in a building as do the organized exchanges such as the New York Stock Exchange

POINT   In stock market terms, one dollar

POOL   An aggregation of capital used to influence stock prices

PORTFOLIO   The list of securities held by an investor or financial house, such as a bank, mutual fund, or investment trust

PYRAMID   Any financial structure, personal or corporate, that uses a small amount of capital to finance much larger operations

RIGGING   Any activity intended to change stock prices that is not based on genuine buying and selling

SEAT   In stock market terms, membership of an exchange

SECURITIES AND EXCHANGE COMMISSION (SEC)   Agency responsible for overseeing the stock market, a financial policeman

SELLING SHORT   Selling borrowed securities in the hope of buying back when cheaper

SHARE   The stock of a company is divided into shares

SHORT SALES   Sales of borrowed securities in the hope of buying them back later when cheaper

SPECULATION   The buying and selling of securities in the hope of gaining by relatively quick changes in the market value

SPLIT   A stock is split just as one $5 bill may be split into five $1 bills; no change in intrinsic value occurs

STOCK   Part-ownership of a company on which dividends are paid

STOP ORDER   An order given to a stockbroker to buy or sell a stock when a certain price is reached; usually referred to as a stop-loss order, since stop orders are often used for that purpose

TAPE   The ribbon of security prices coming out of the ticker

TICKER   The machine that prints the tape giving prices of securities

TRICKLE DOWN   A reference to the giving of government aid to industry and finance, instead of to the people directly, in the expectation that some relief or benefit will trickle down to the man-in-the-street, or consumer

WAR DEBTS   The debts incurred in World War I by nations that bought arms and food to fight the war

WASH SALES   Bogus security transactions designed to promote public interest

Additional Reading

Allen, Frederick Lewis. *Only Yesterday*. New York: Harper, 1931.
———. *Since Yesterday*. New York: Harper, 1940.
Brooks, John. *Once in Golconda*. New York: Harper & Row, 1969.
Galbraith, John Kenneth. *The Great Crash 1929*. Boston: Houghton Mifflin, 1961.
Smith, Howard R. *Economic History of the United States*. New York: Ronald Press, 1955.

Index

148